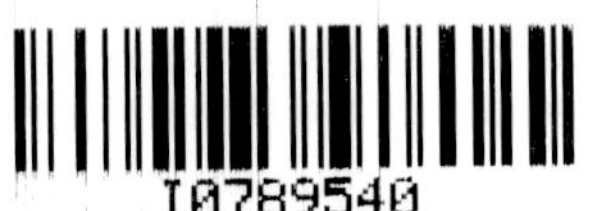

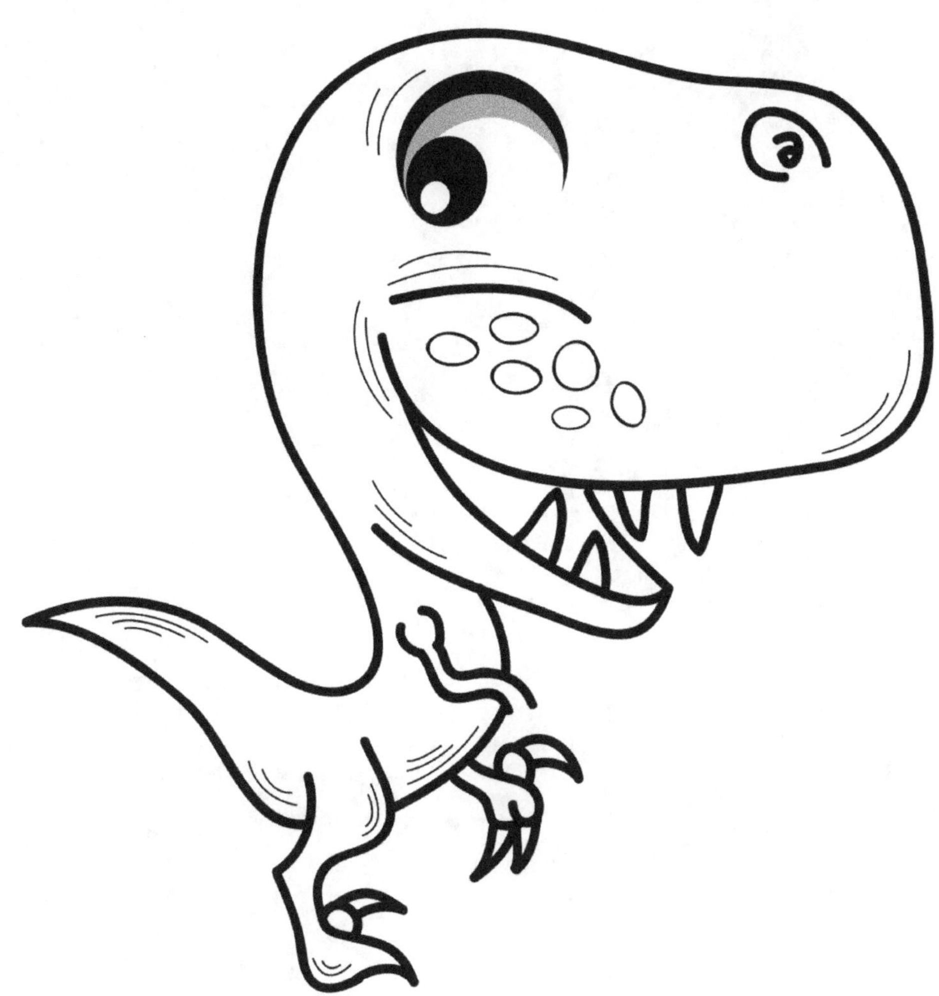

This Coloring Book belongs to.....

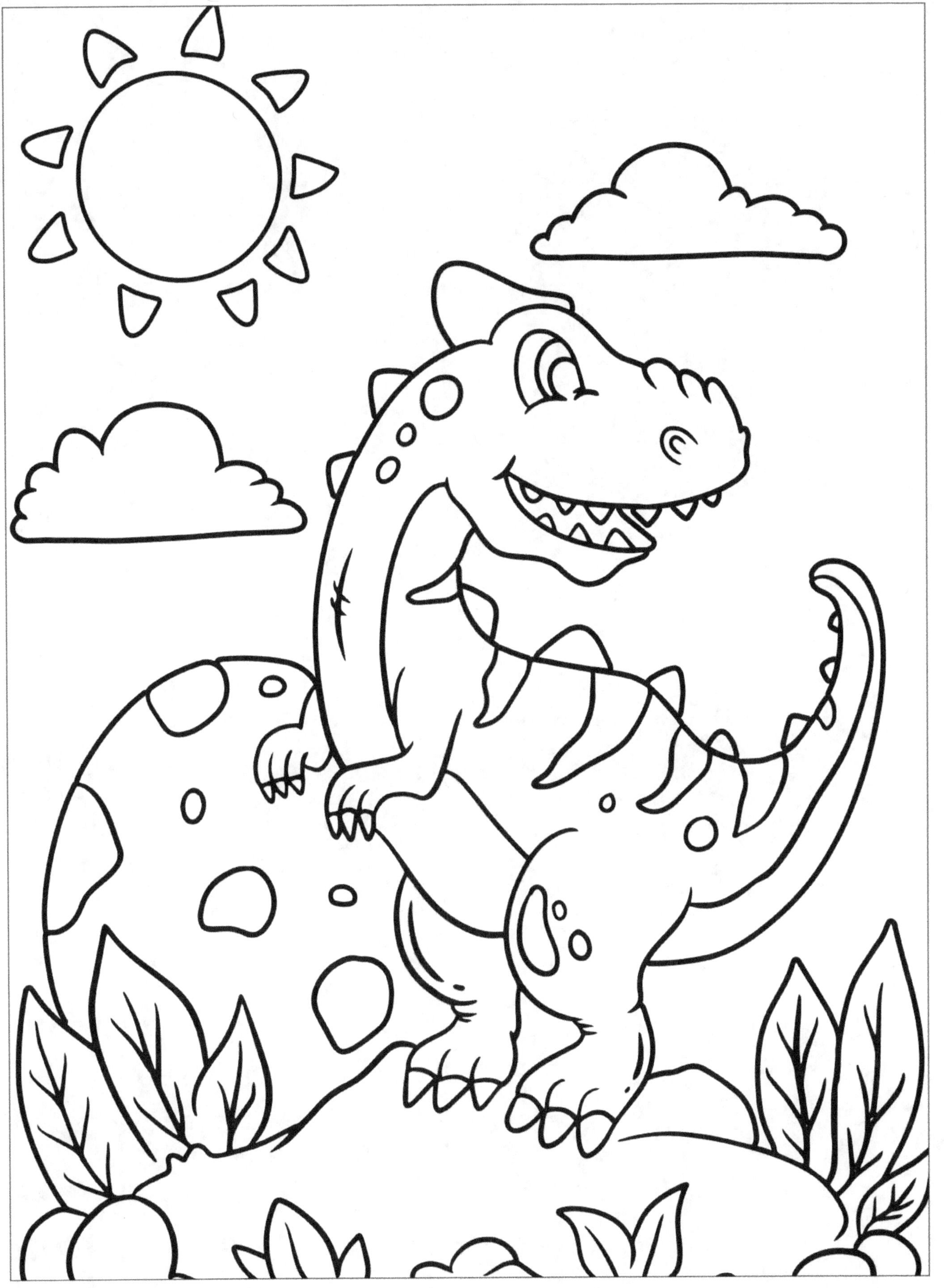

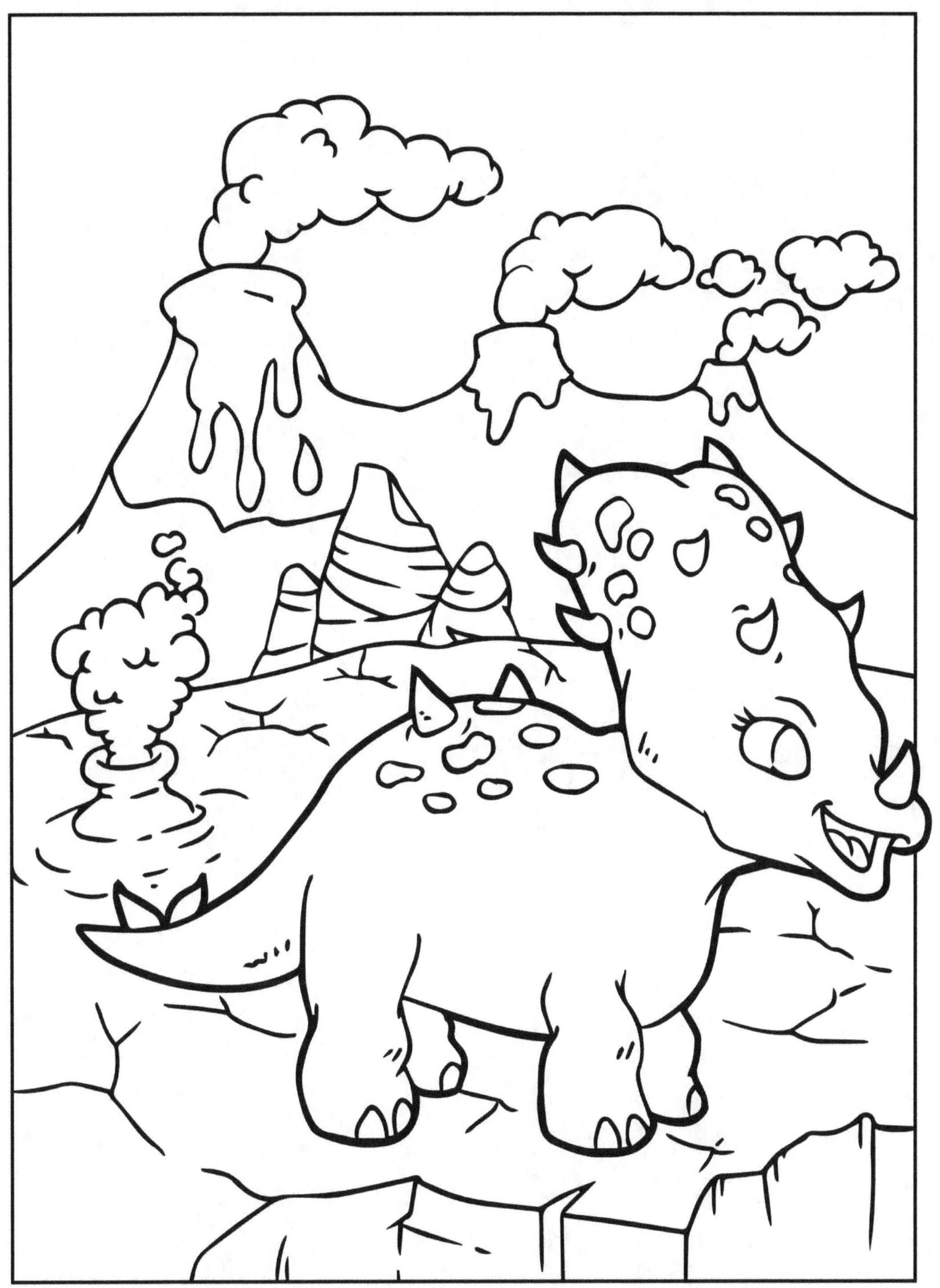

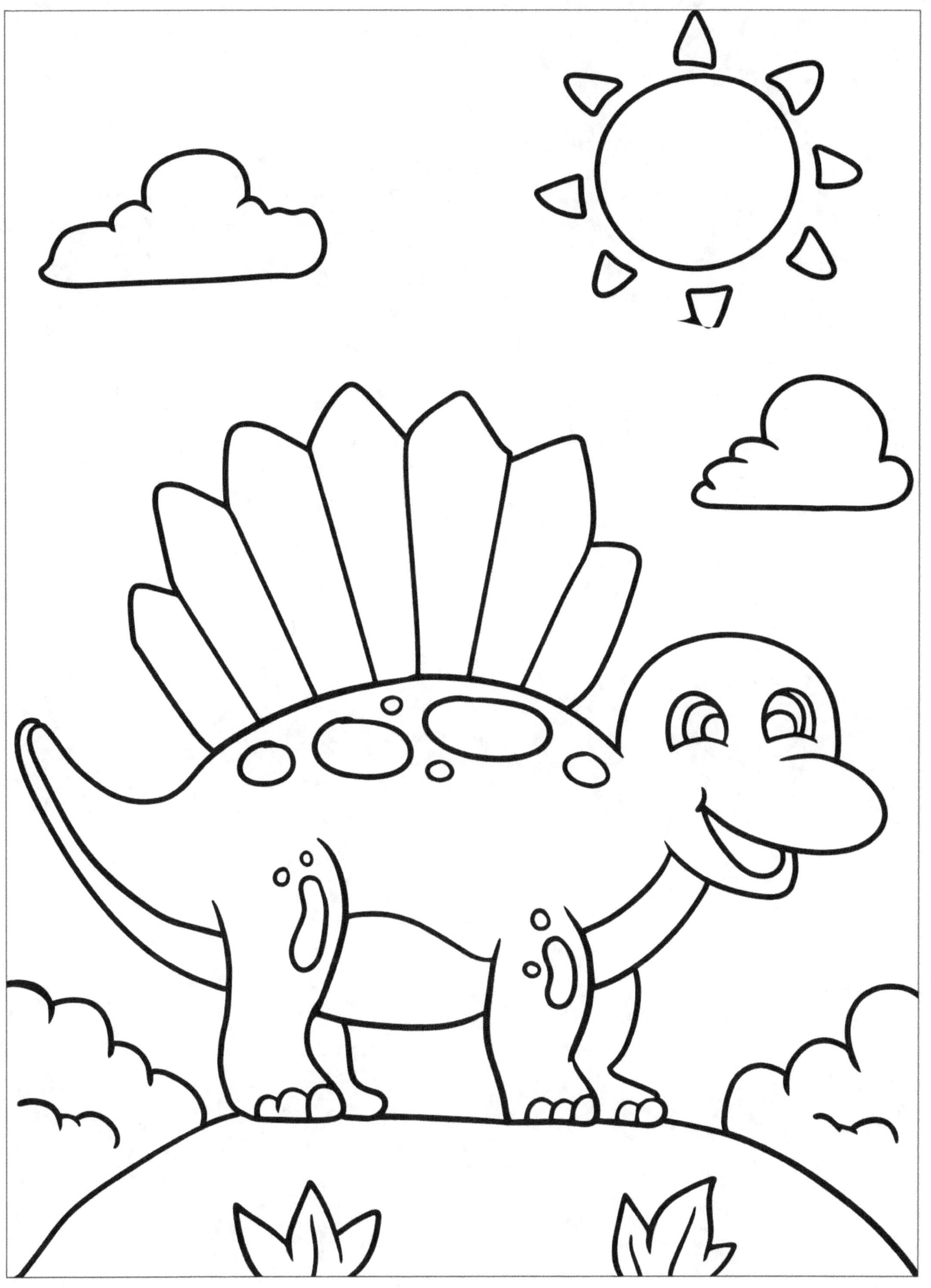

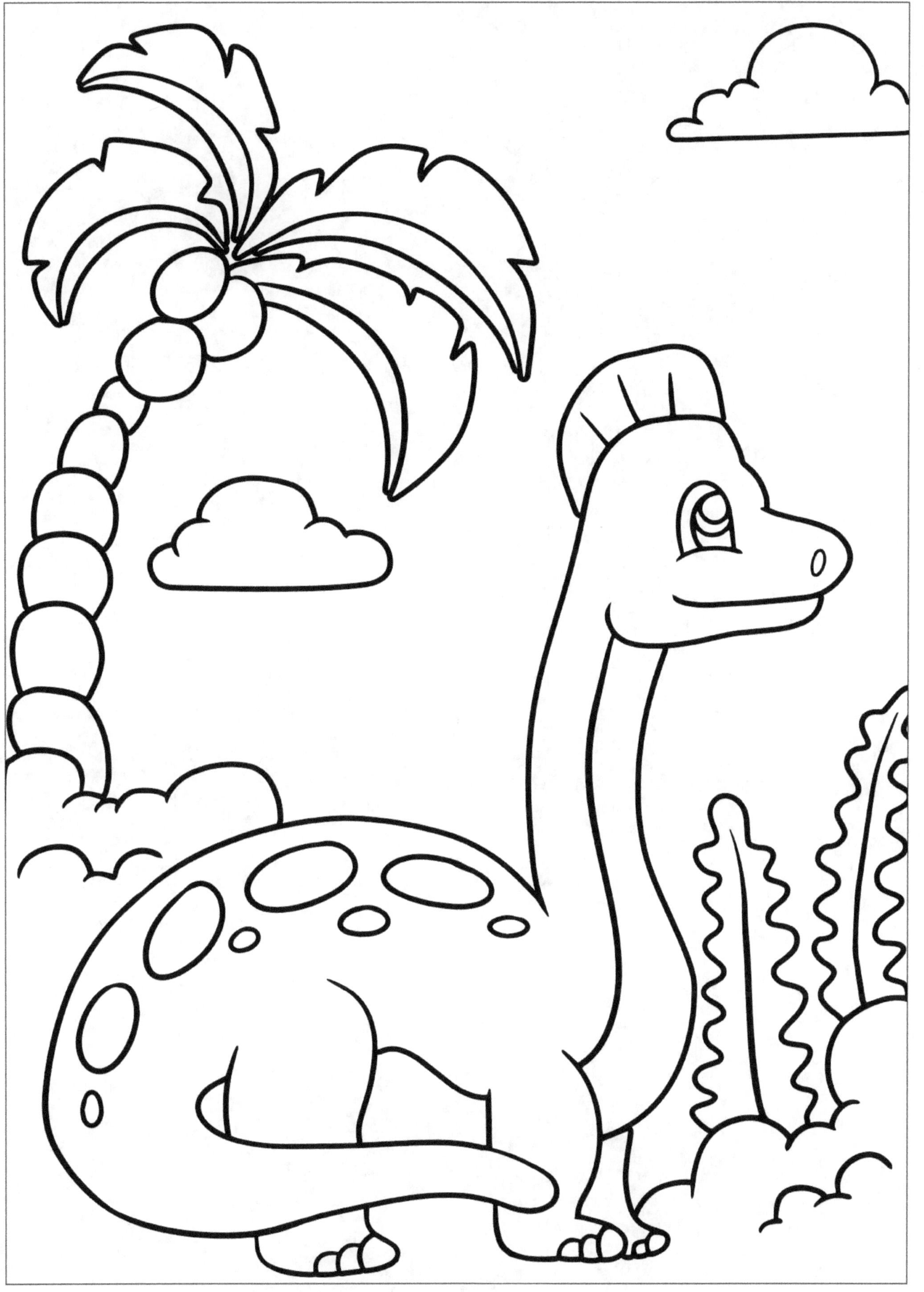

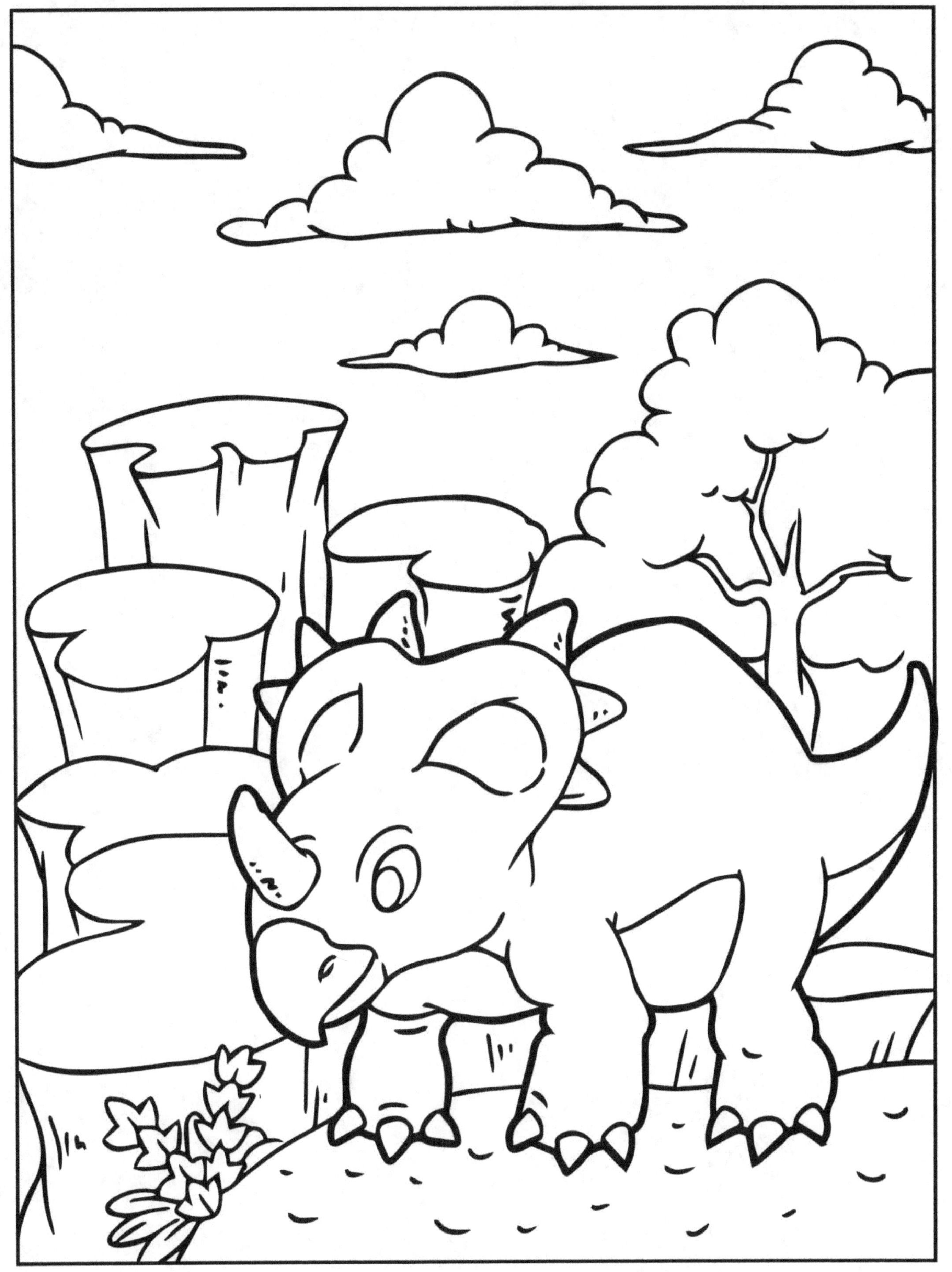

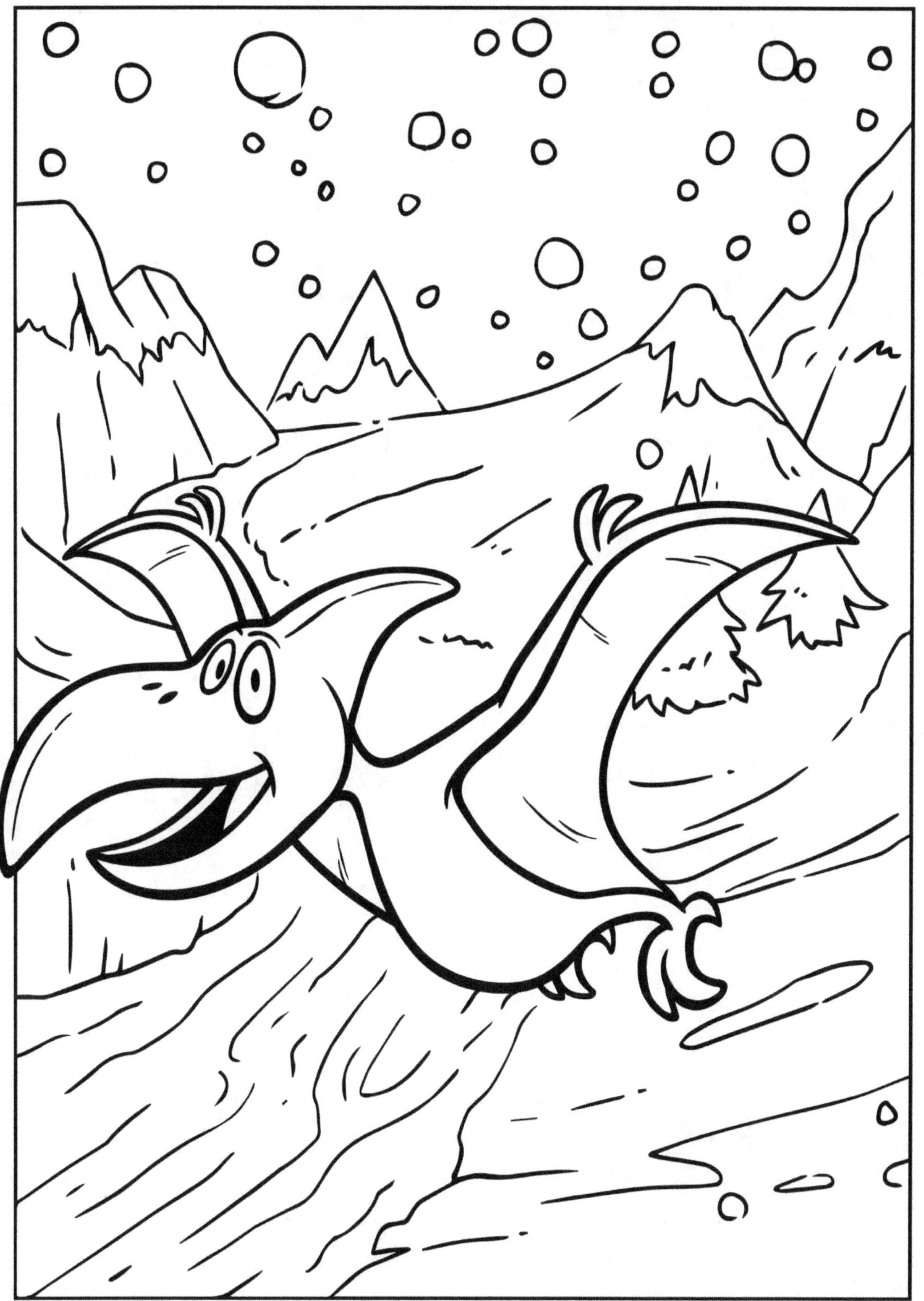

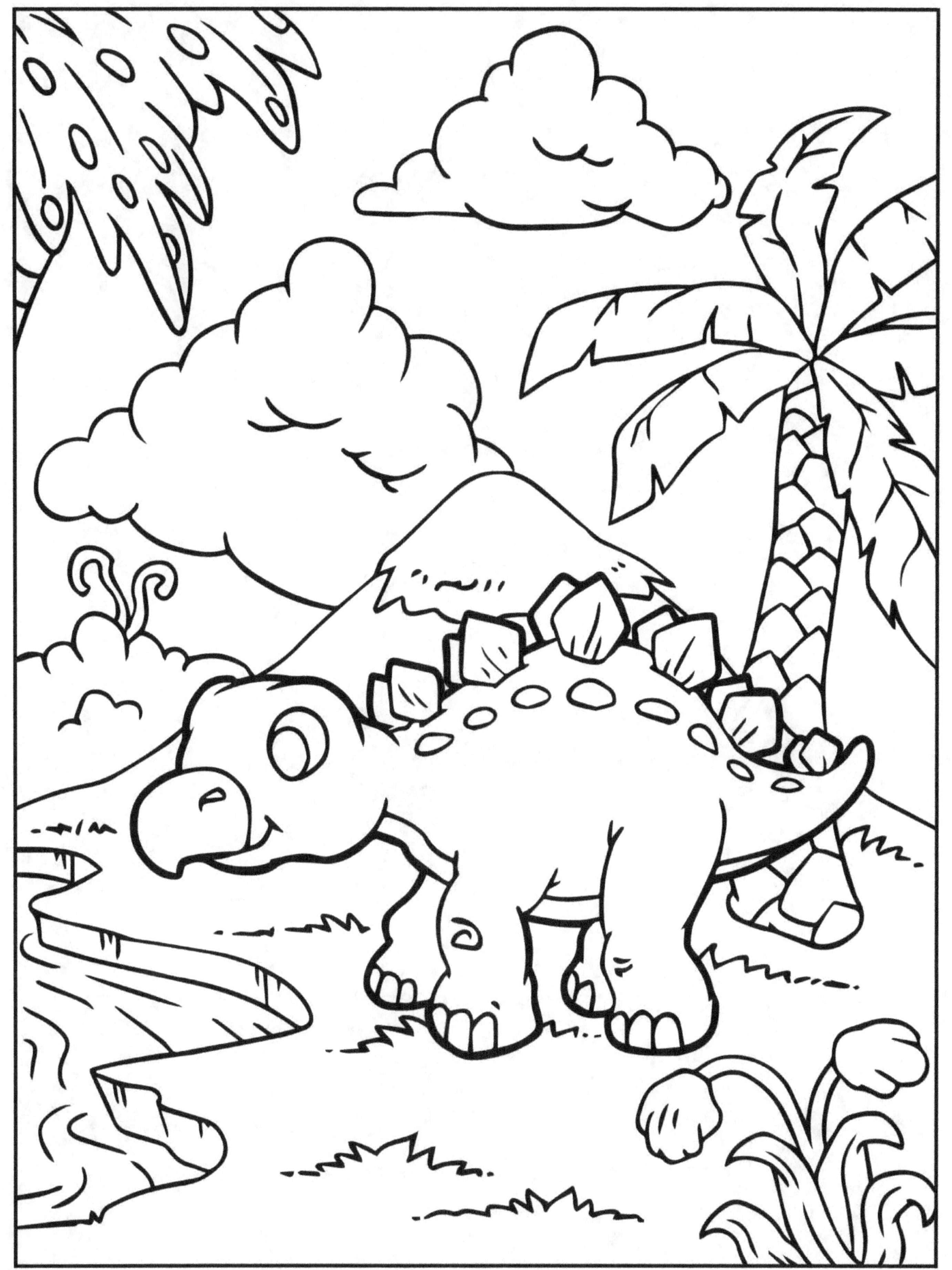

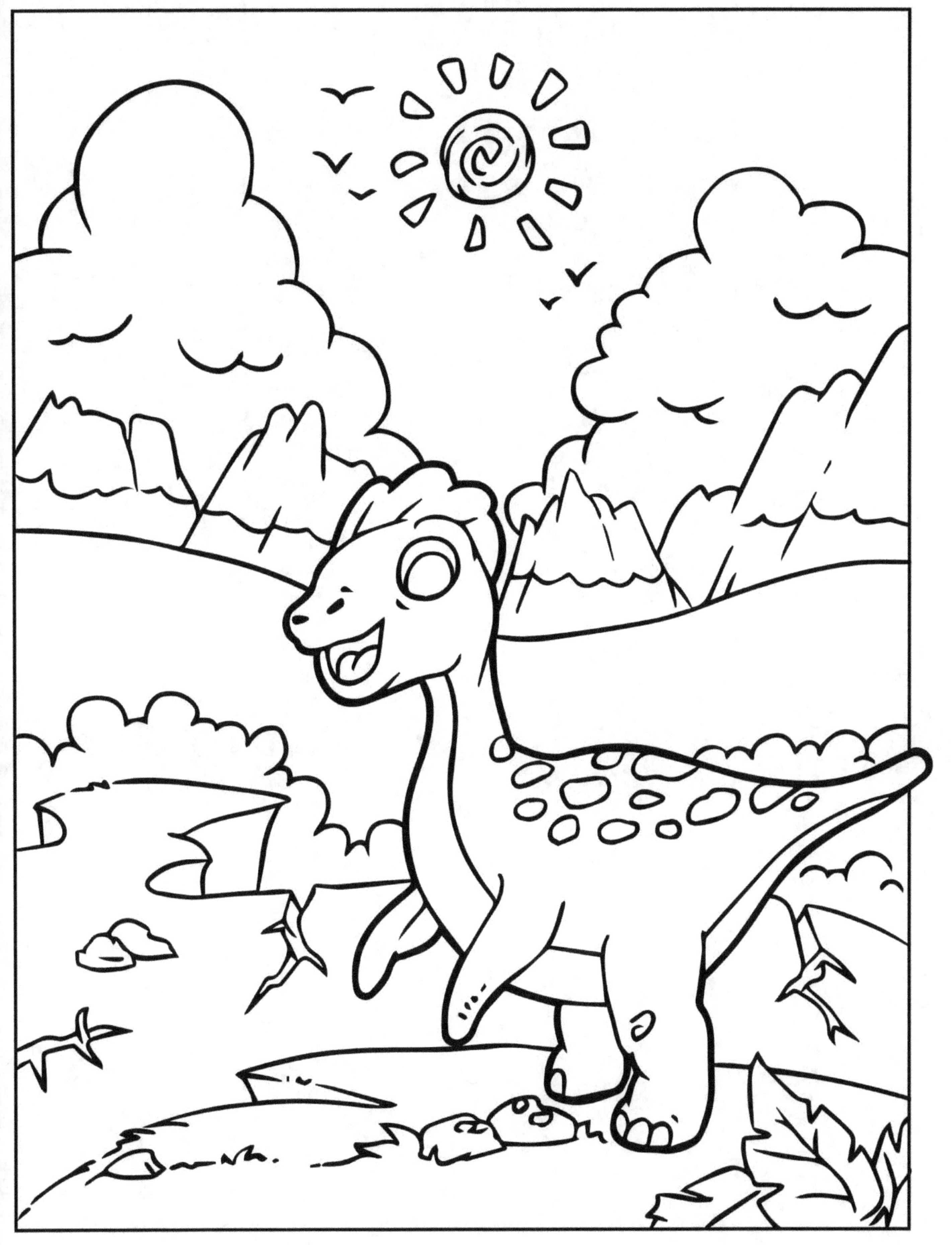

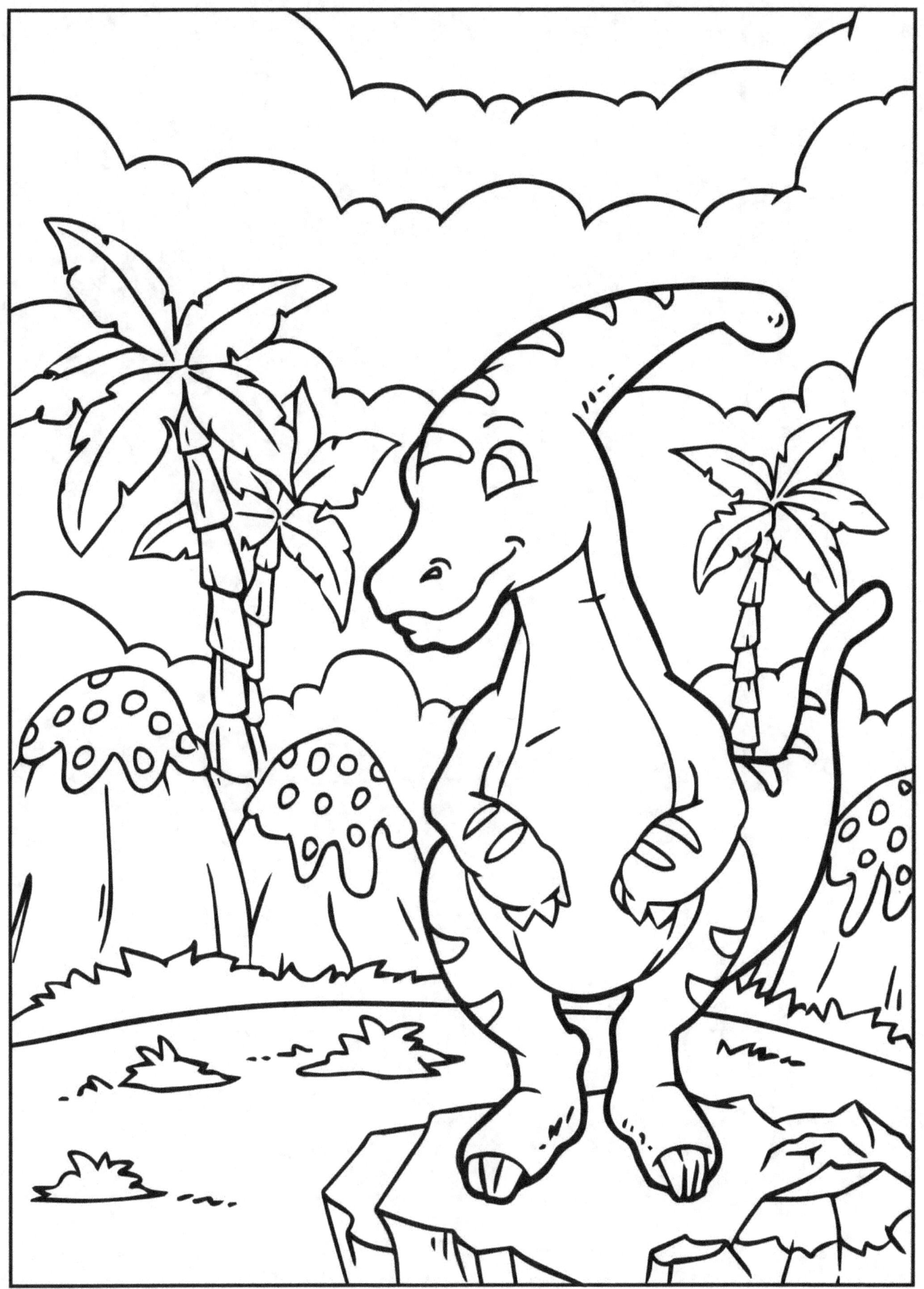

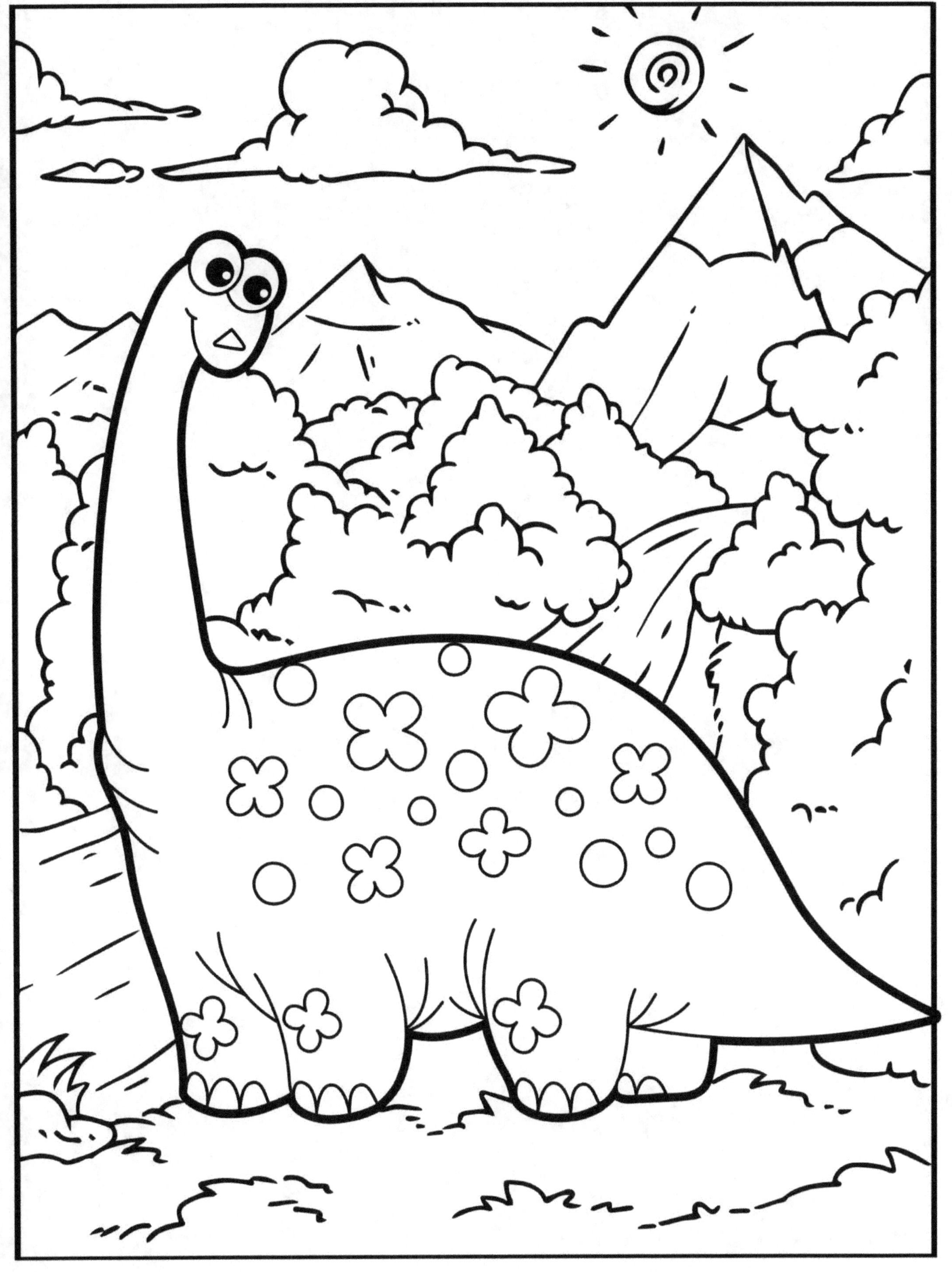

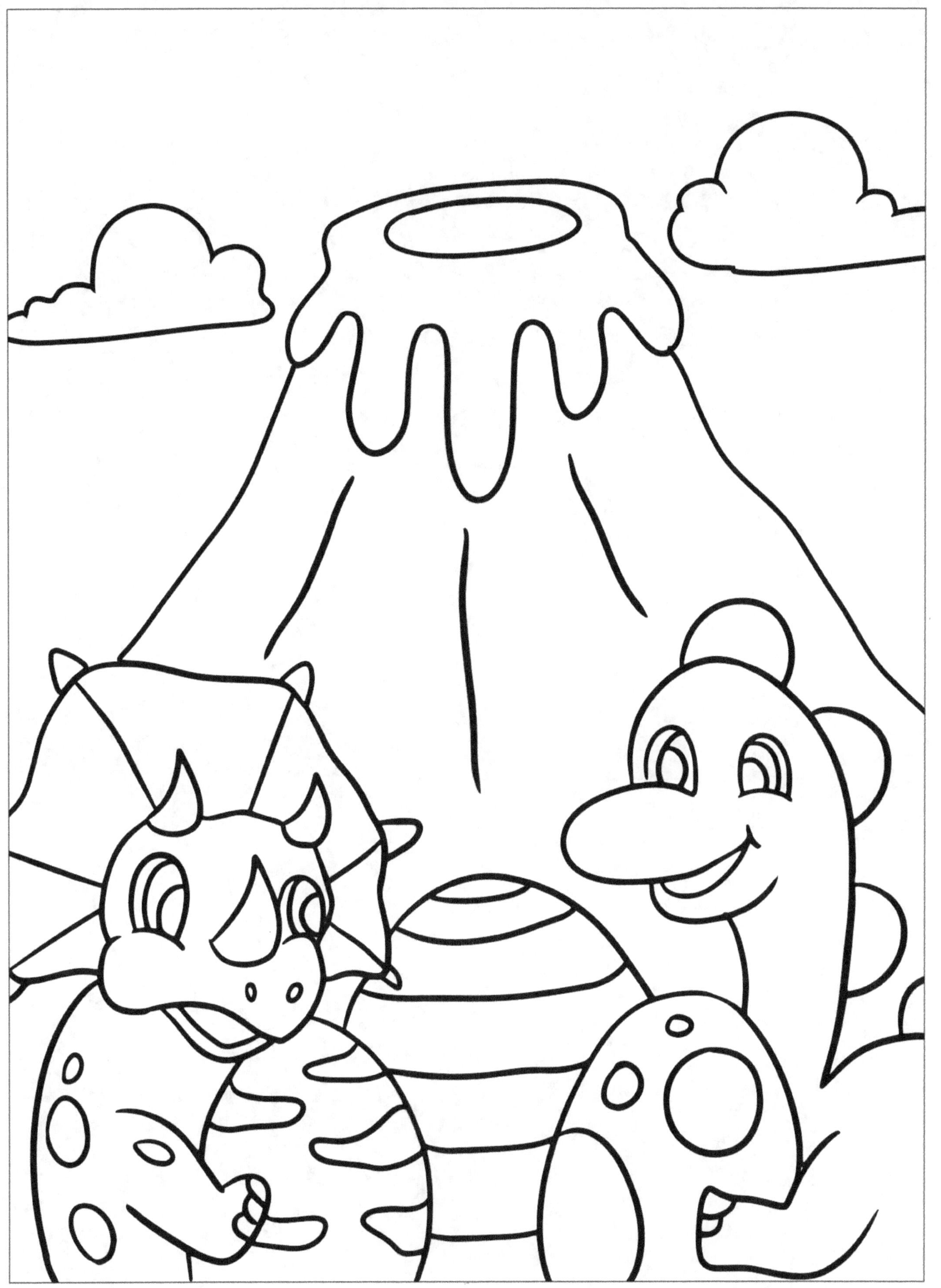

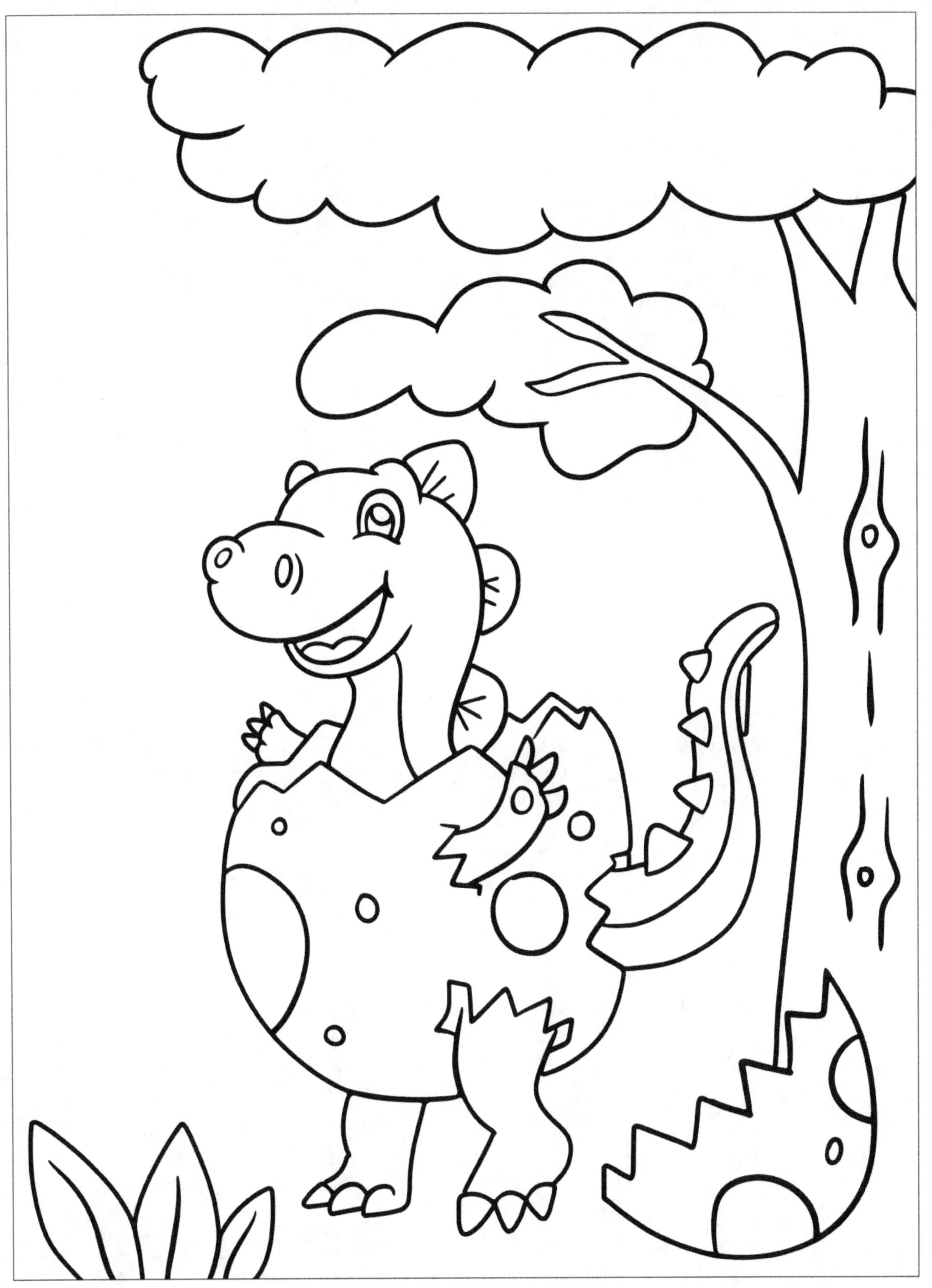

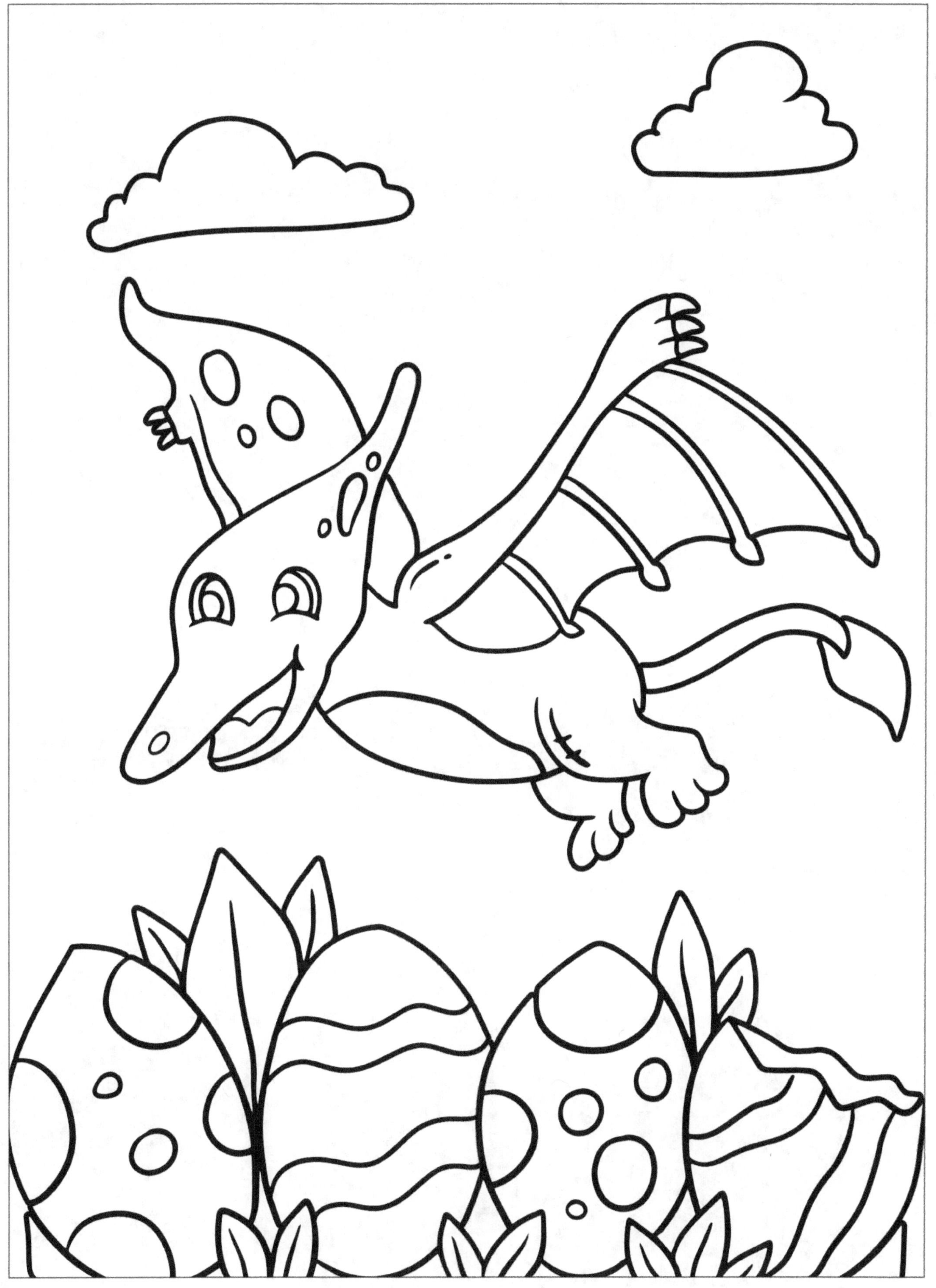

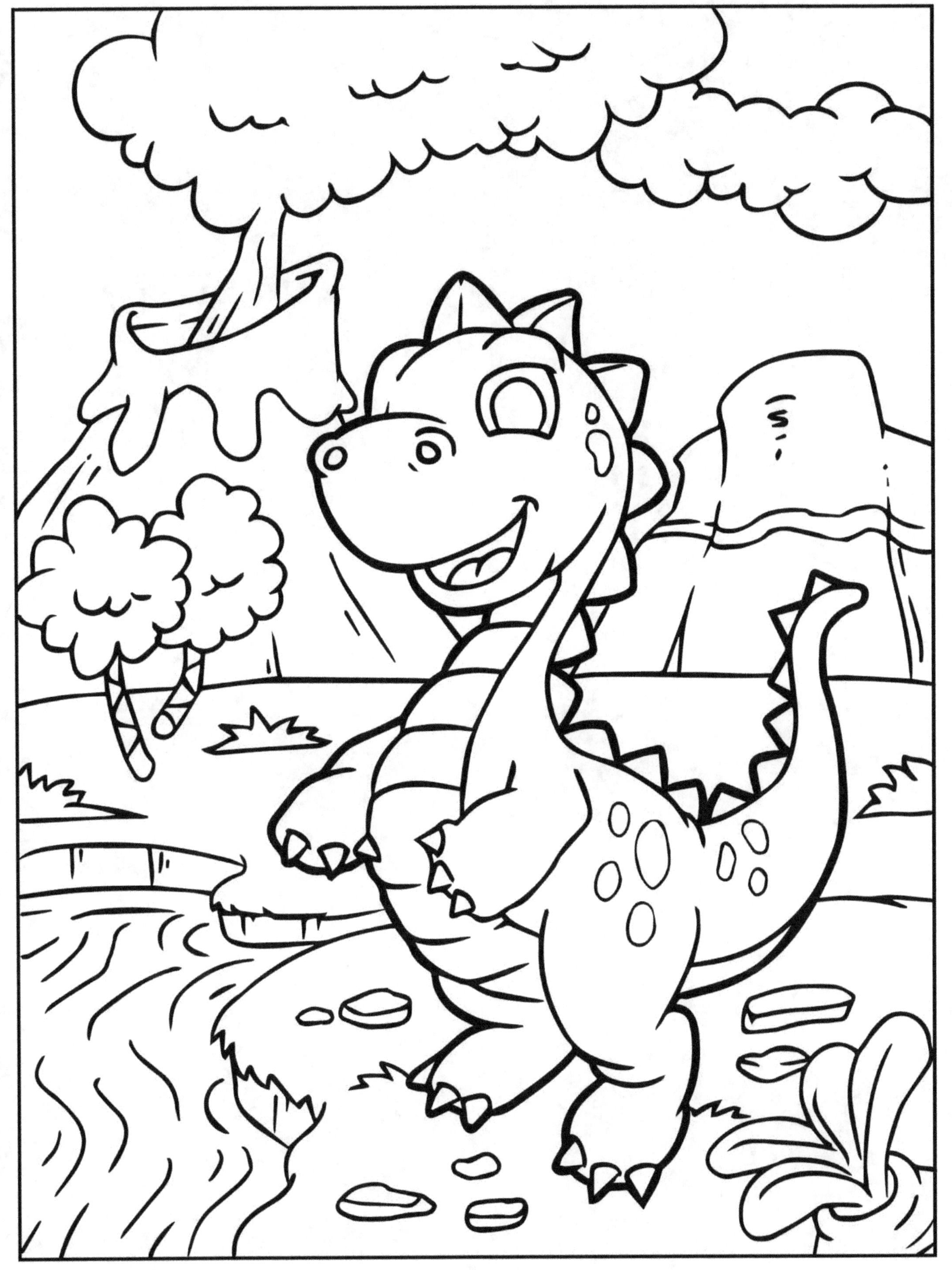

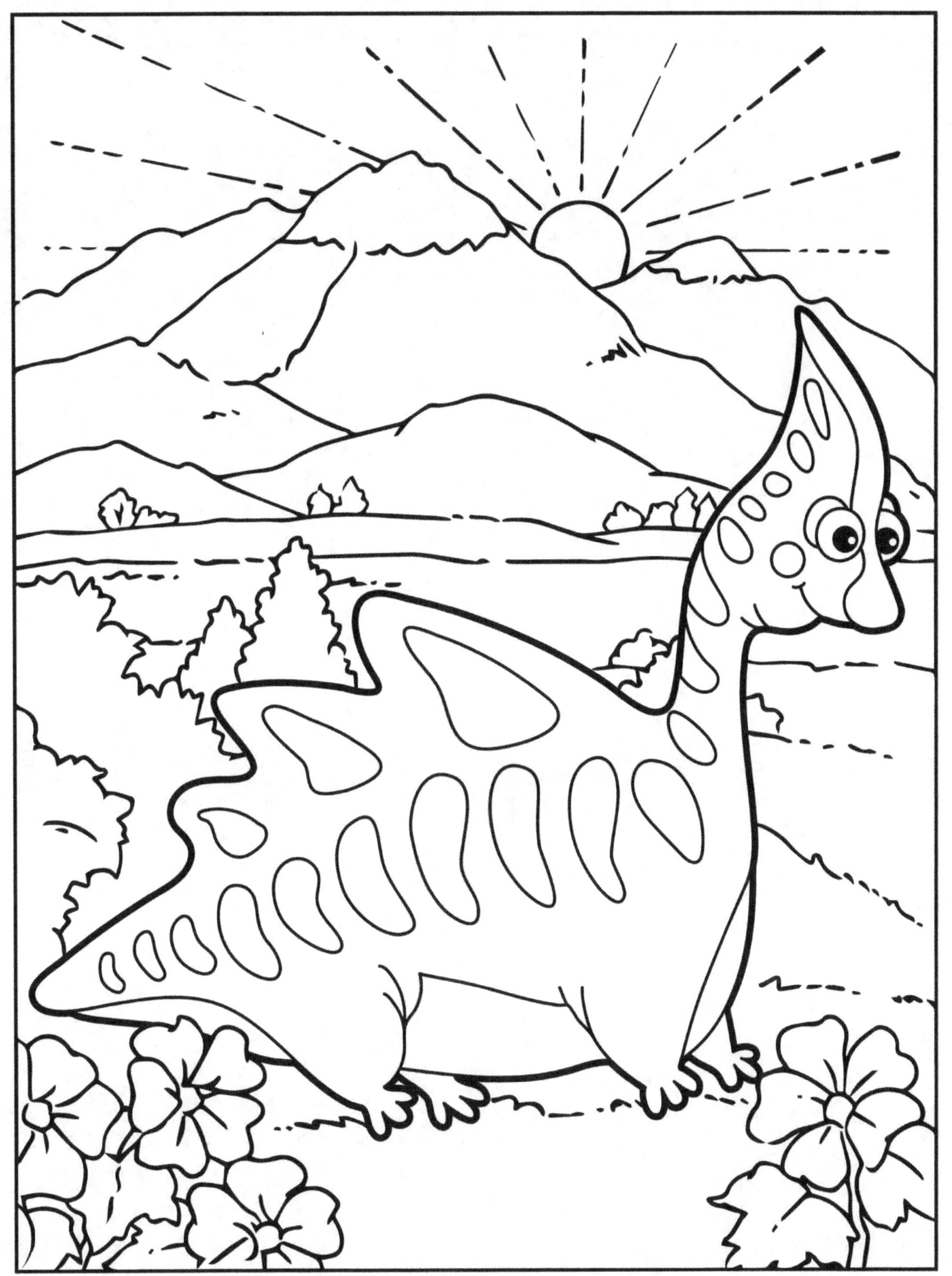

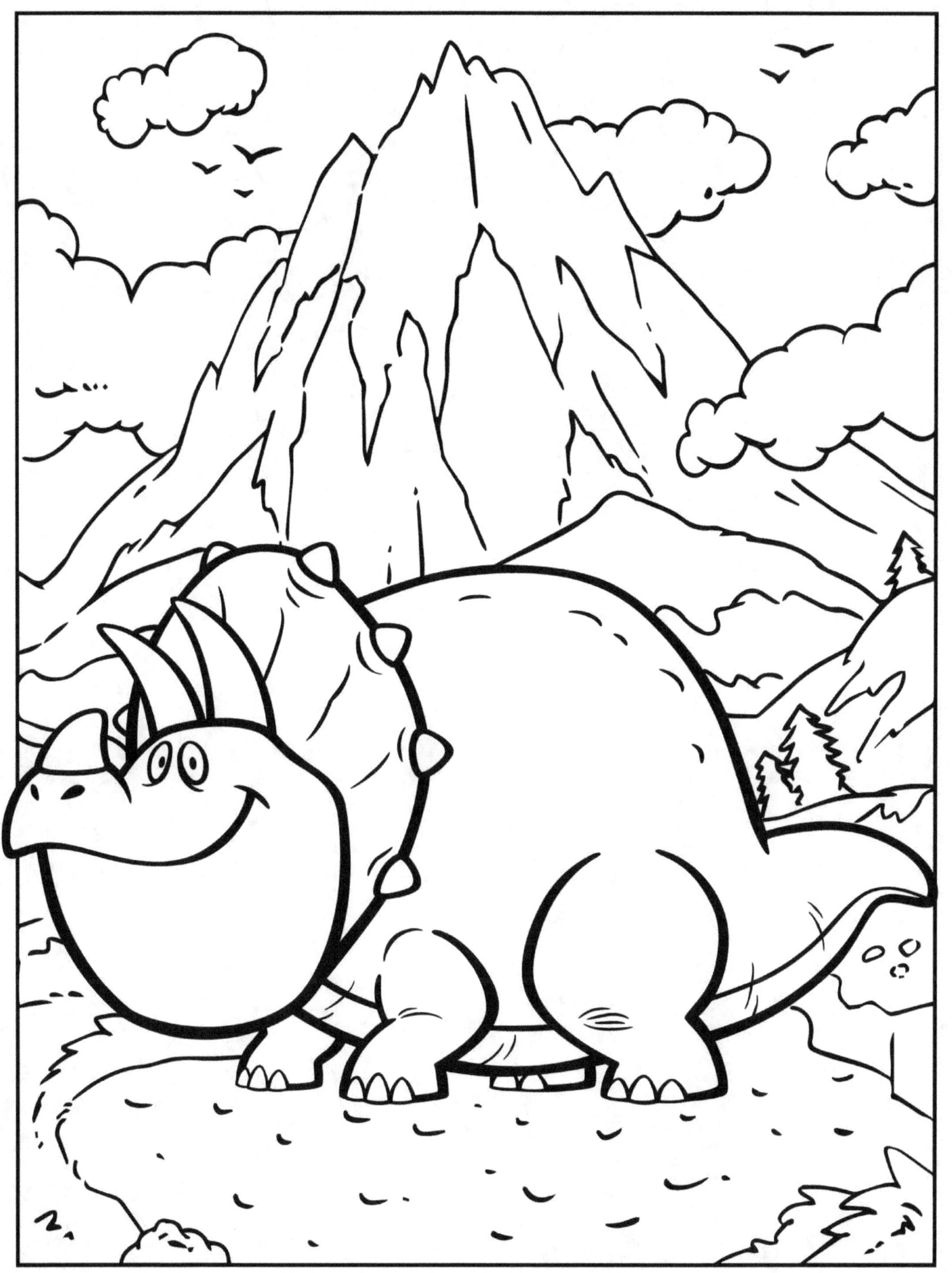

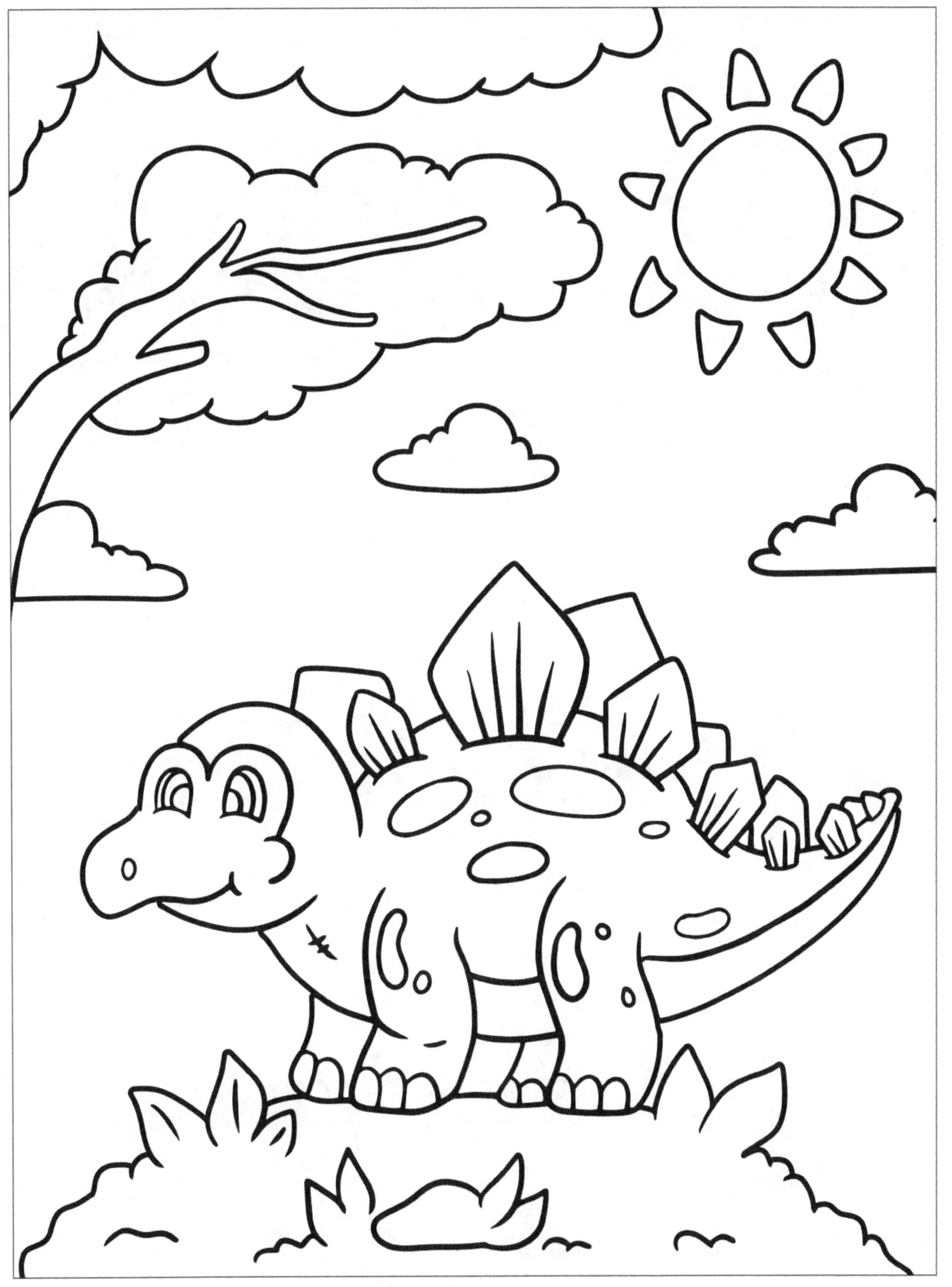

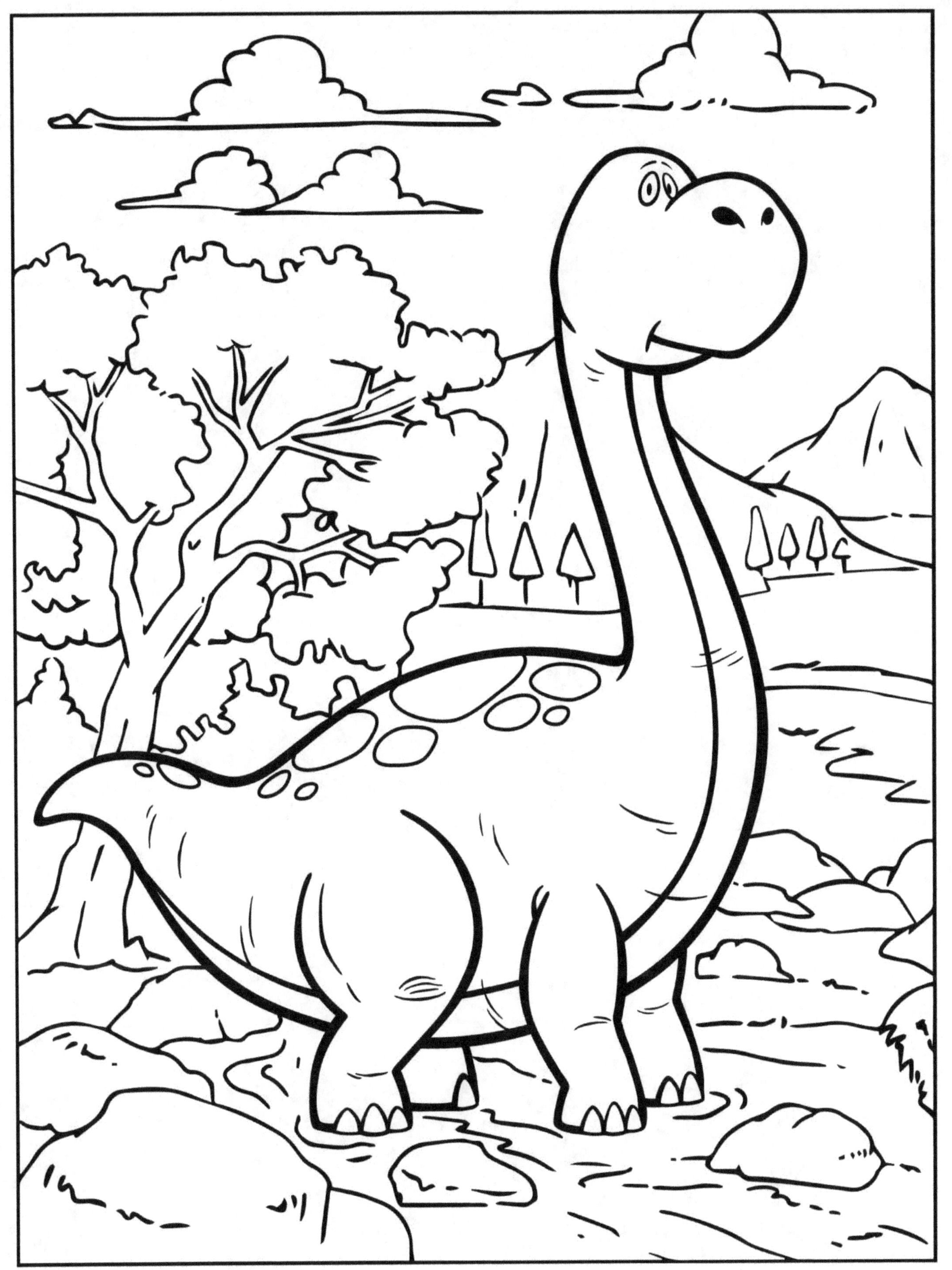

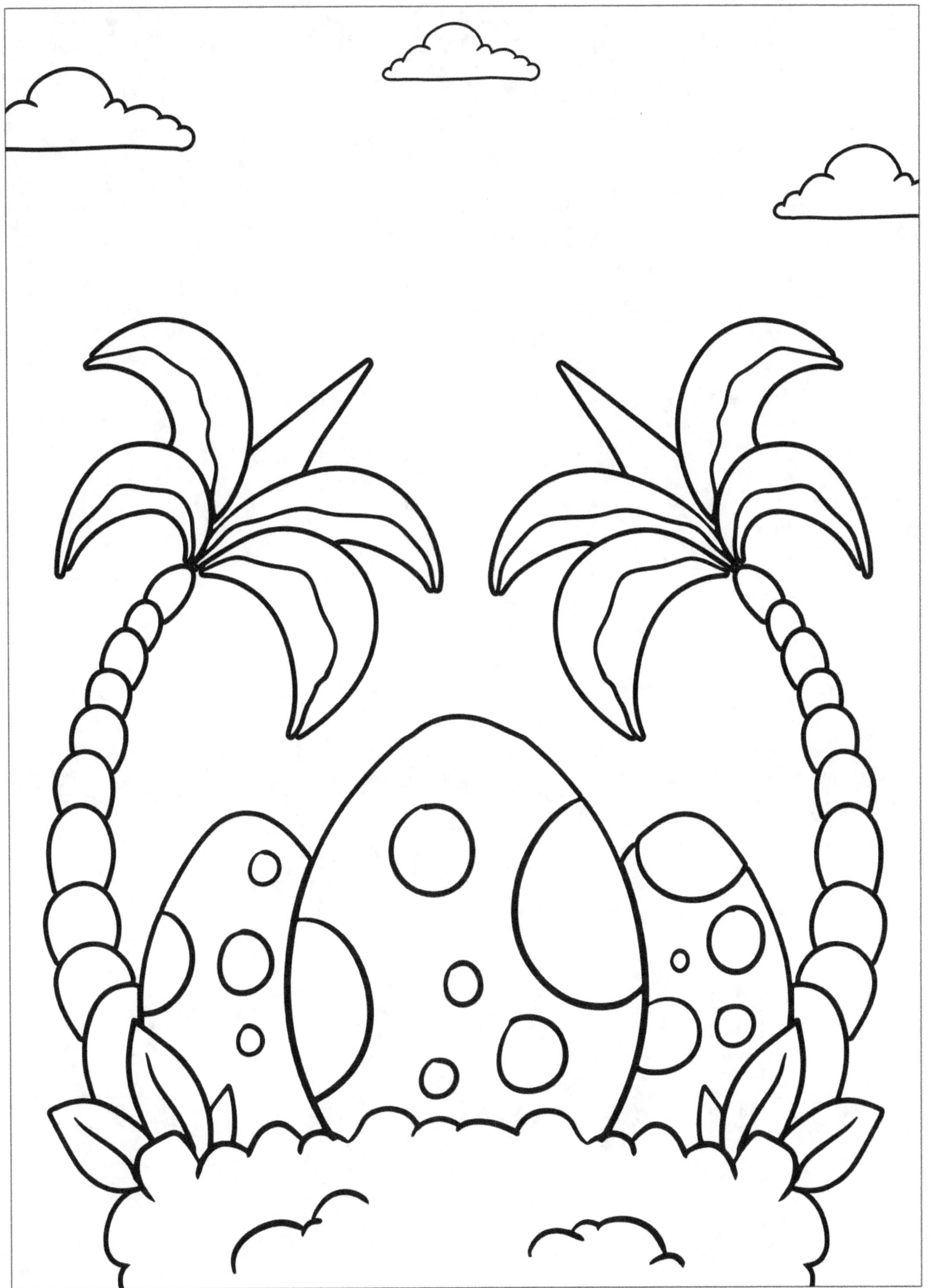

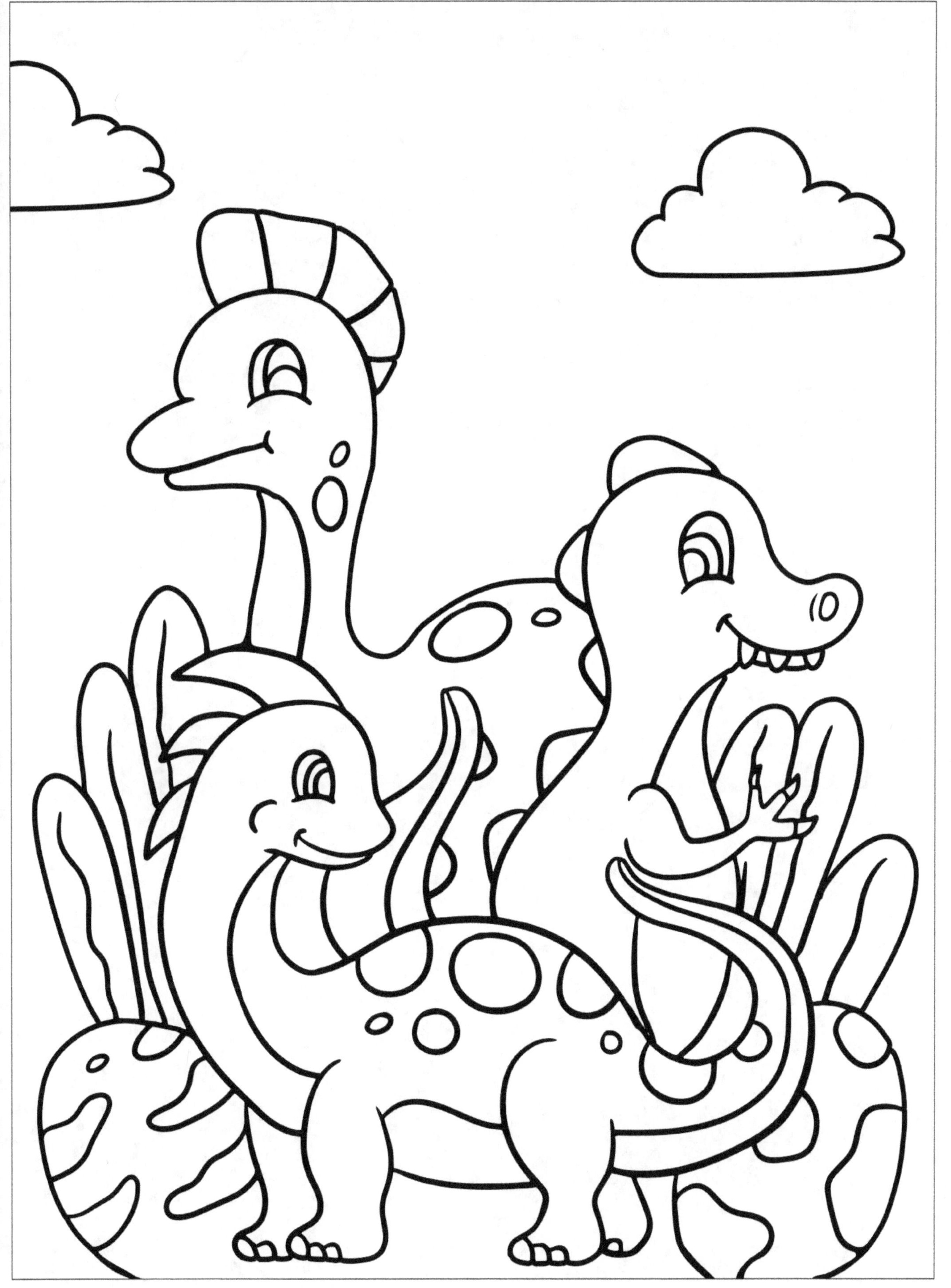

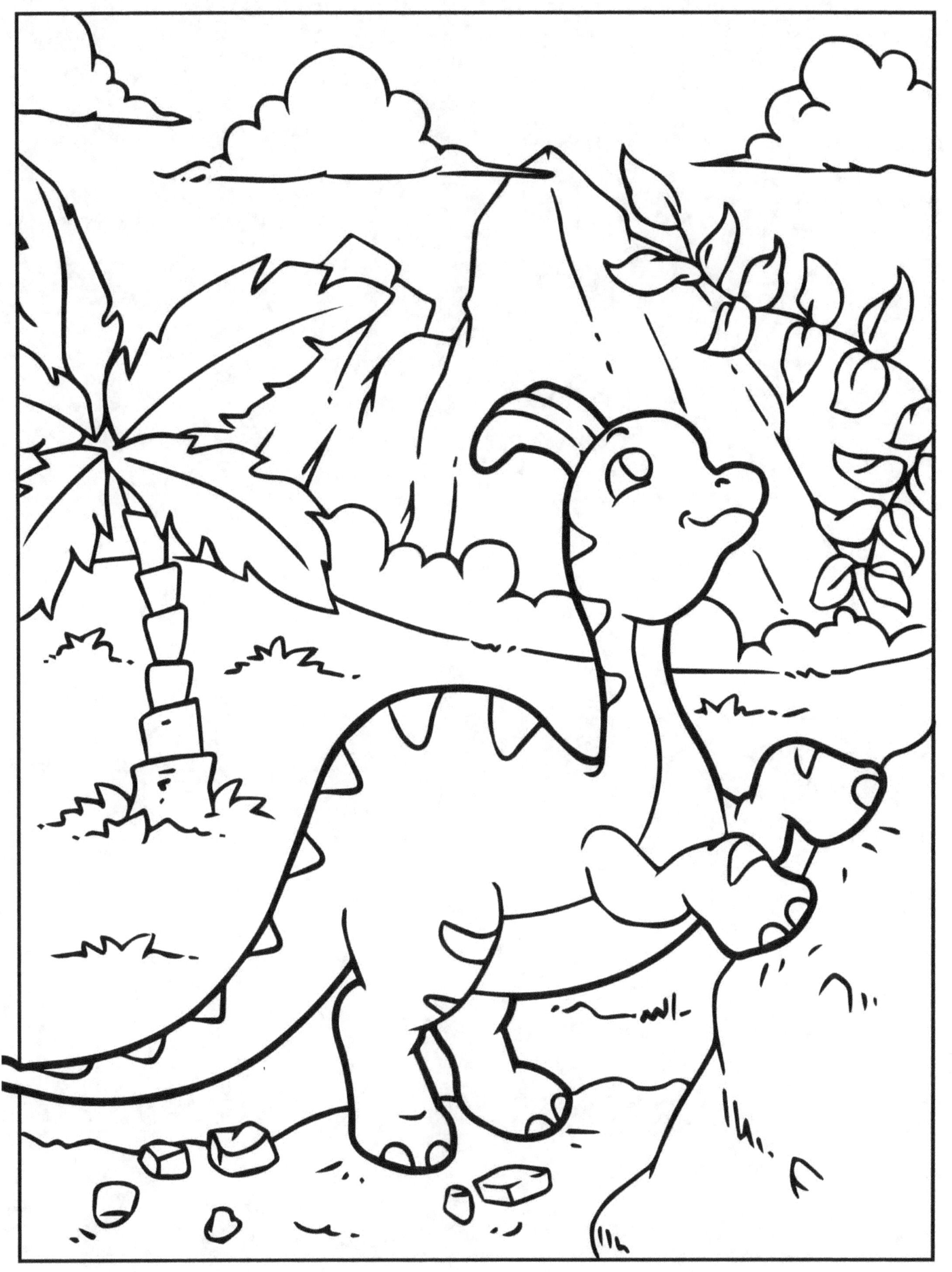

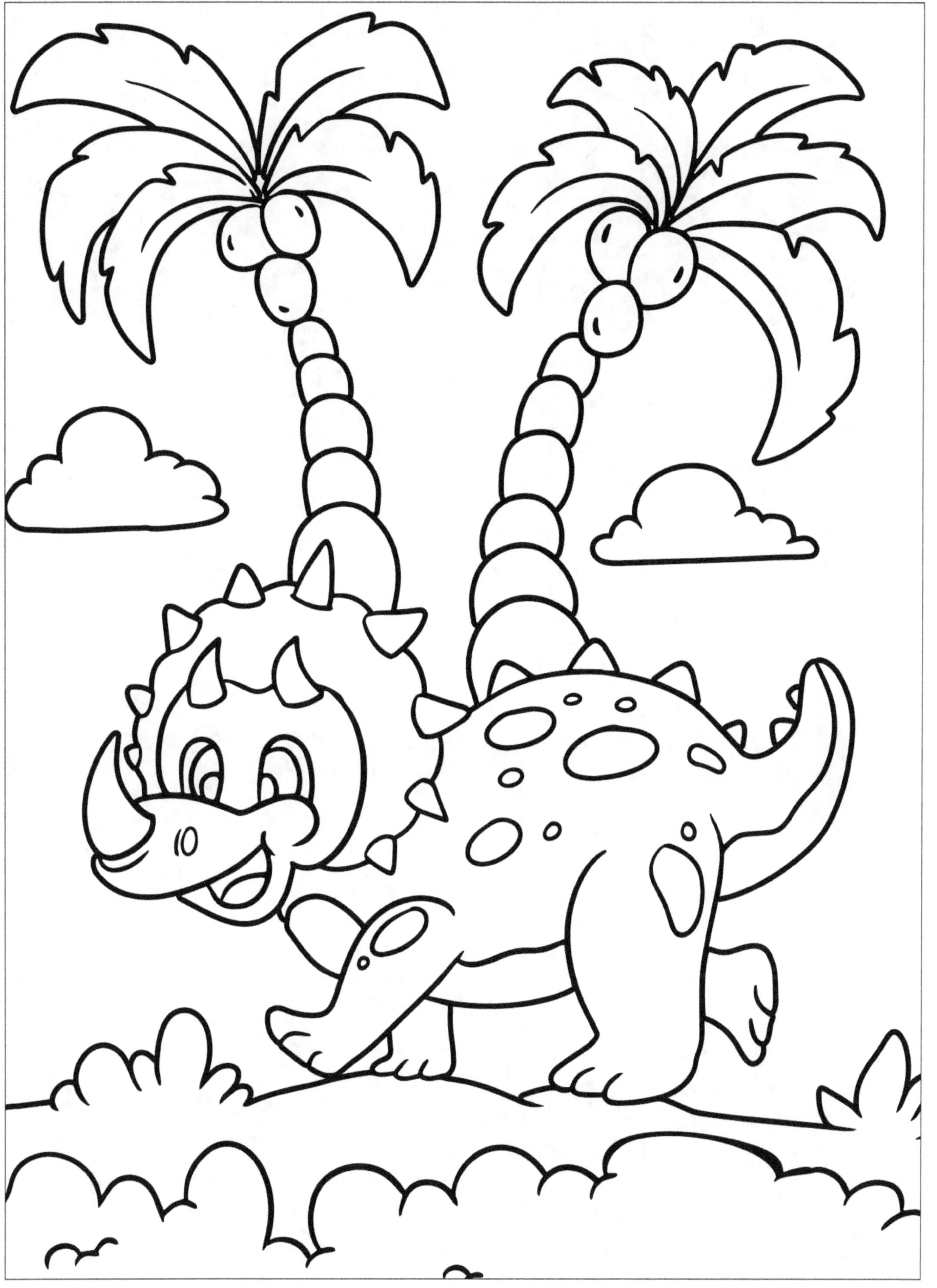

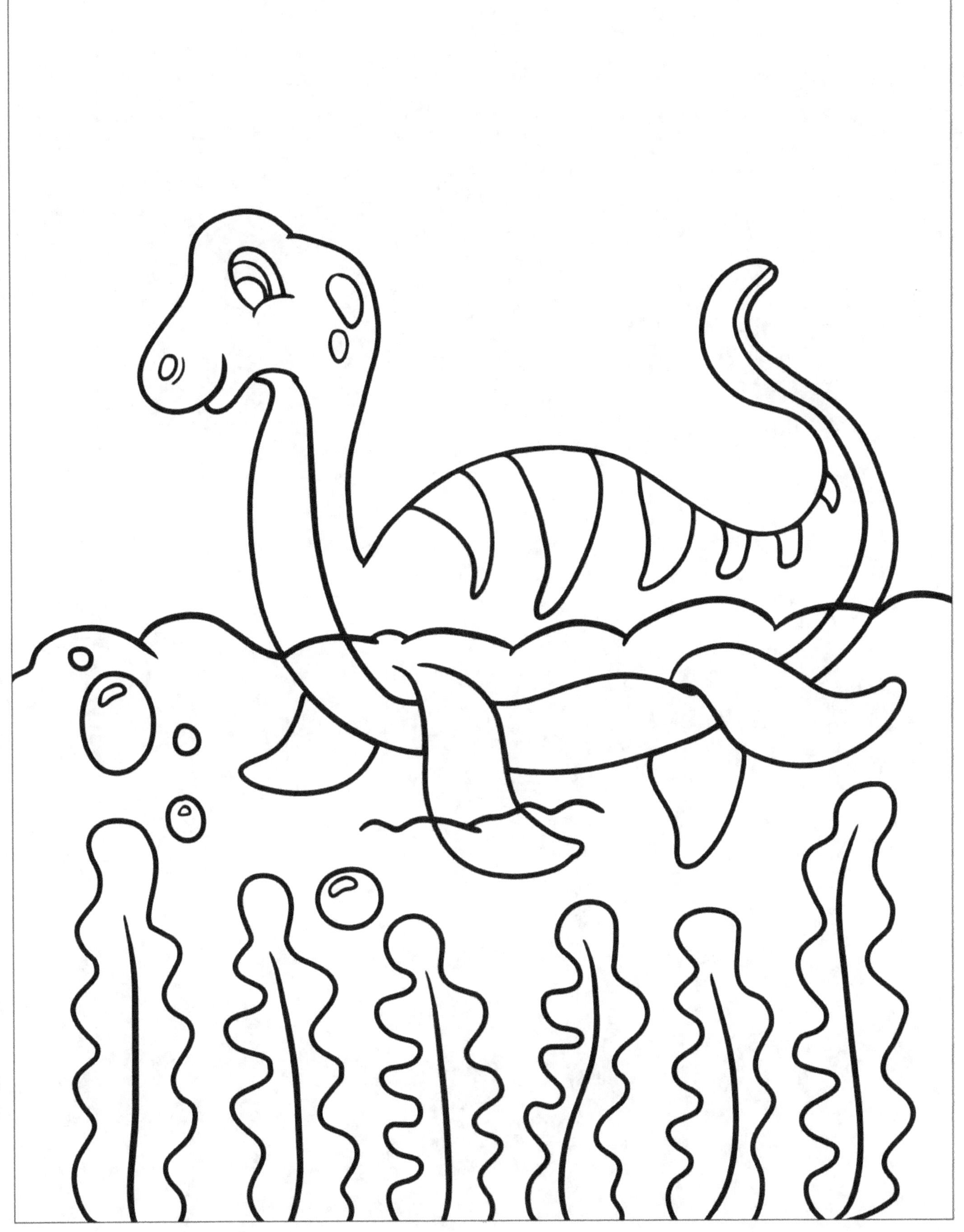

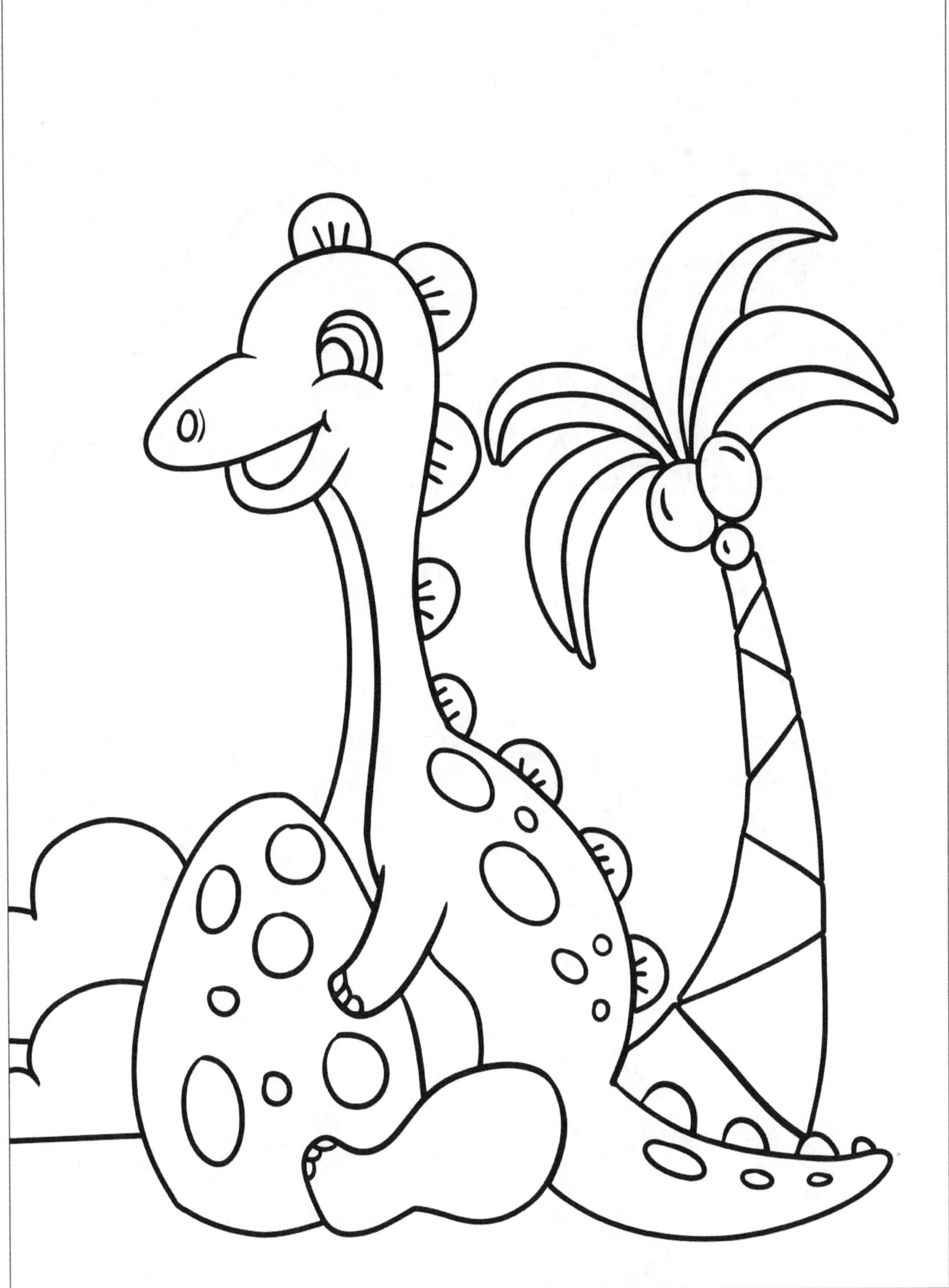

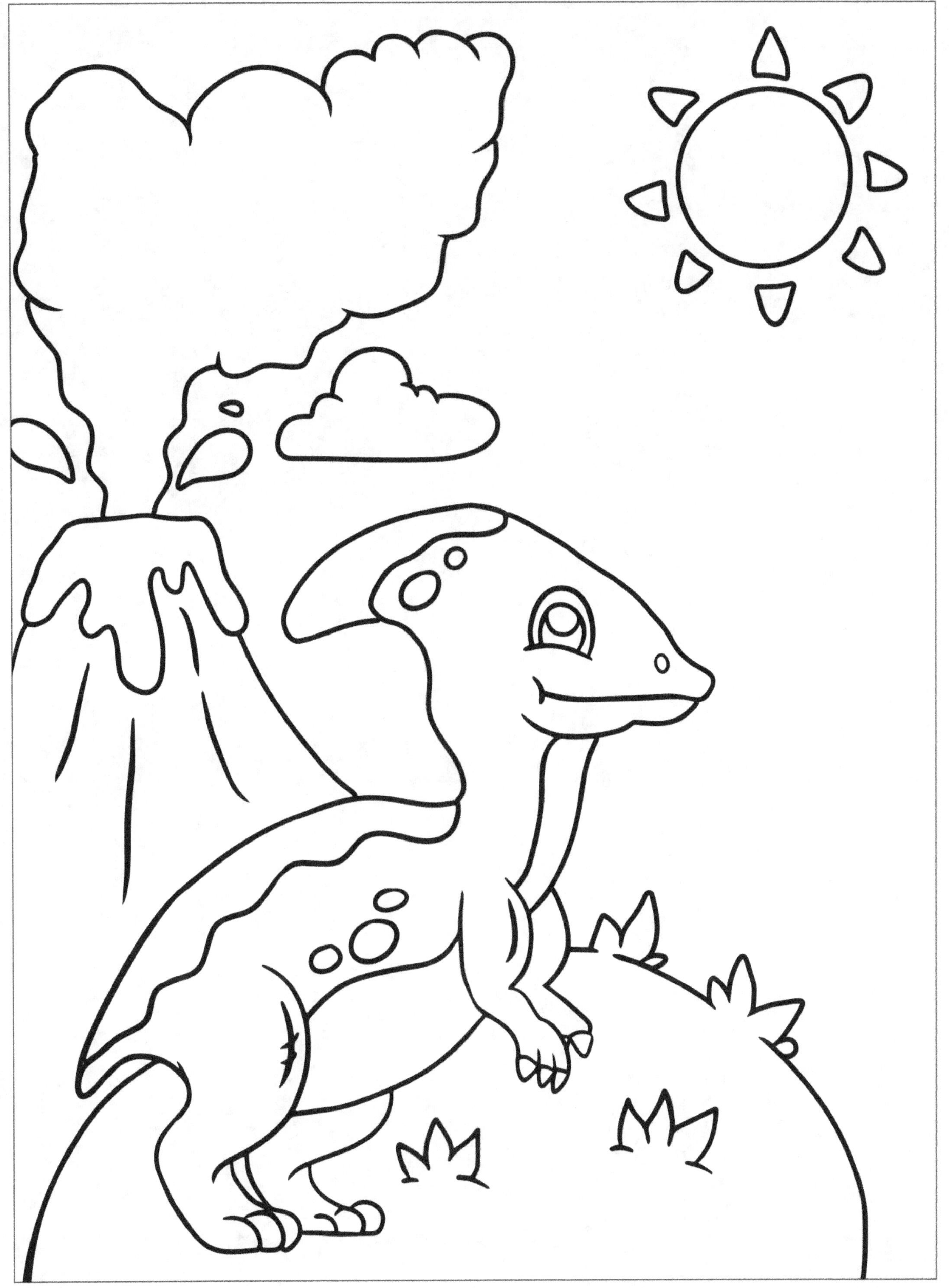

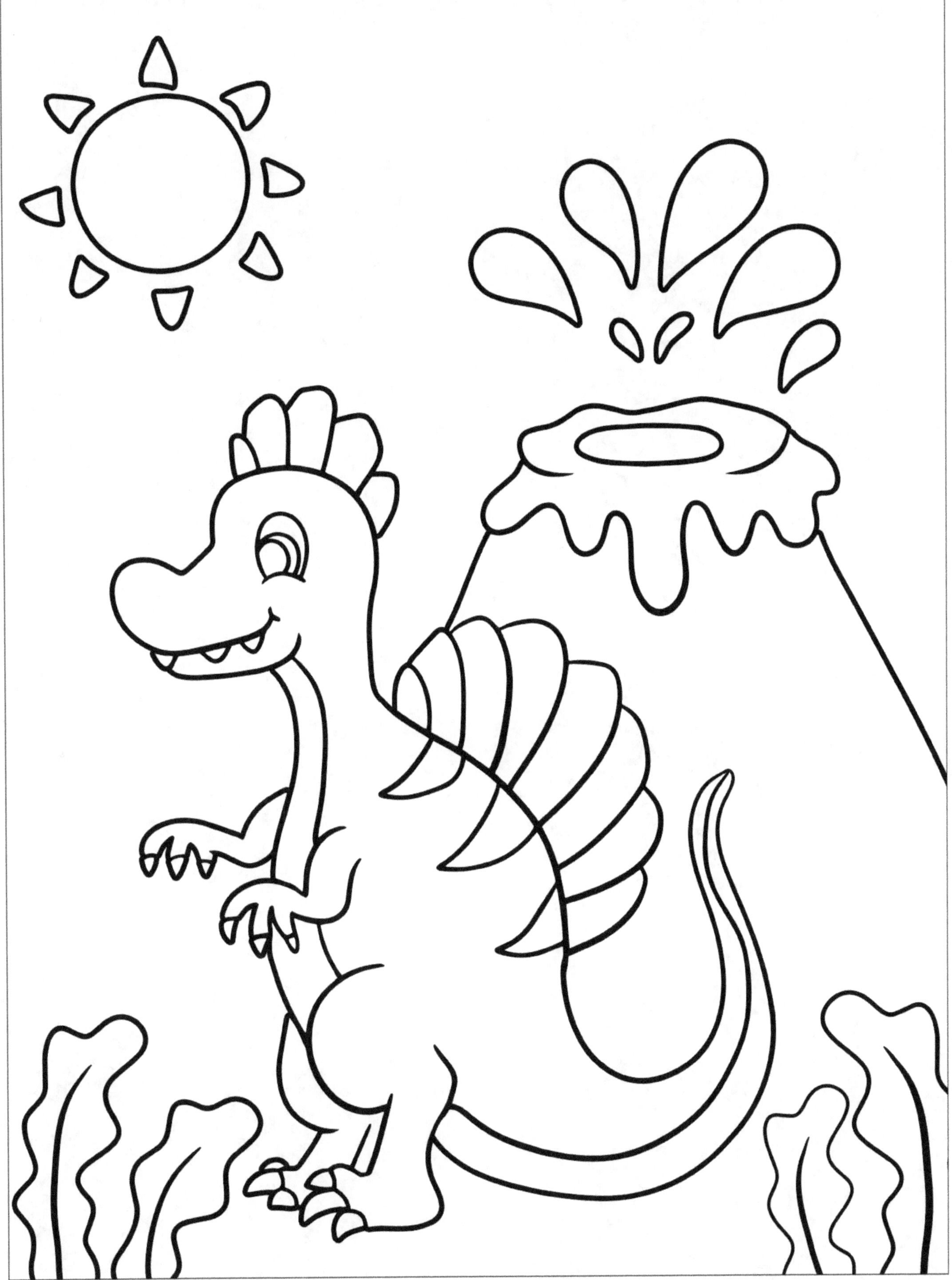

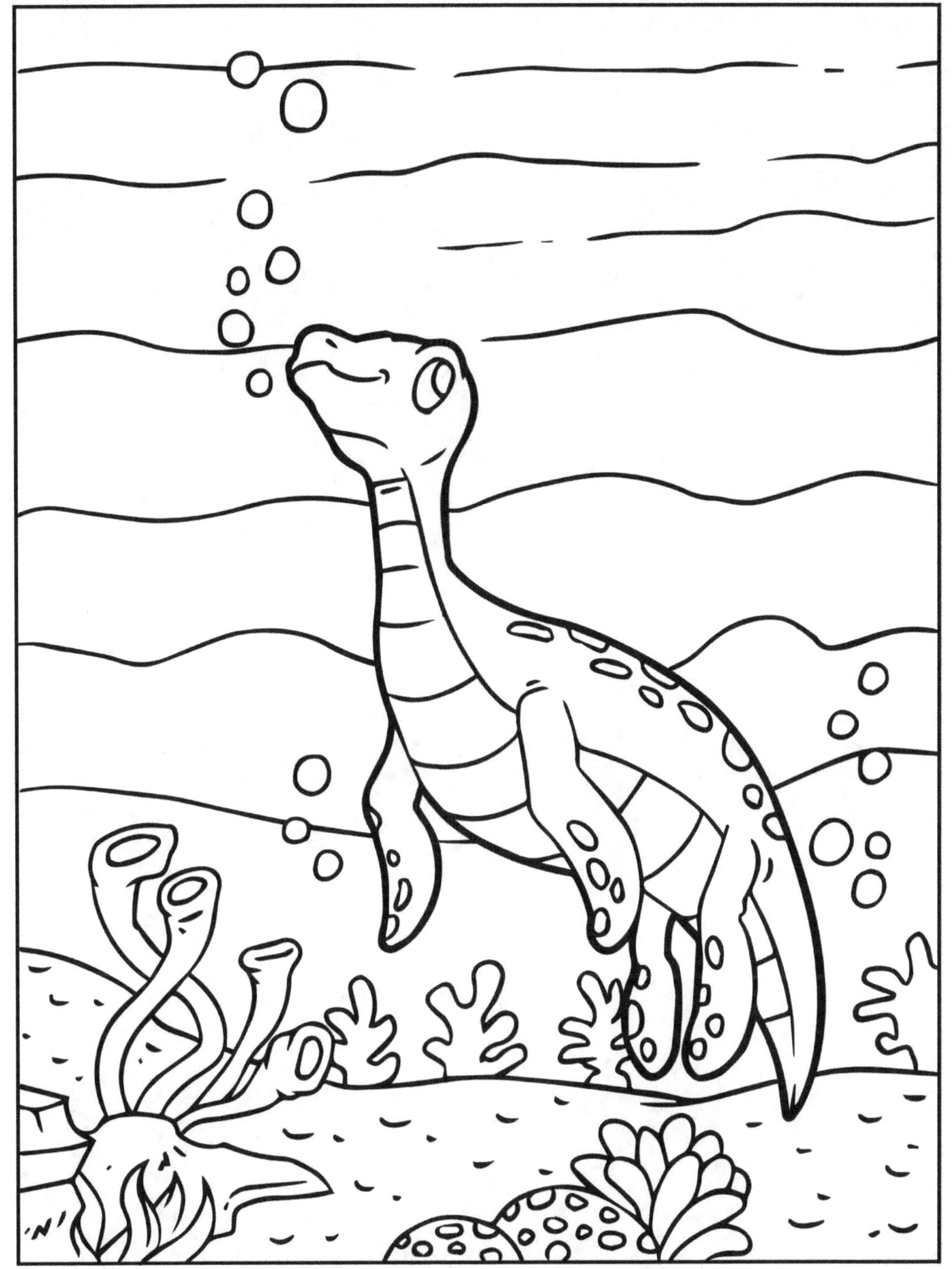

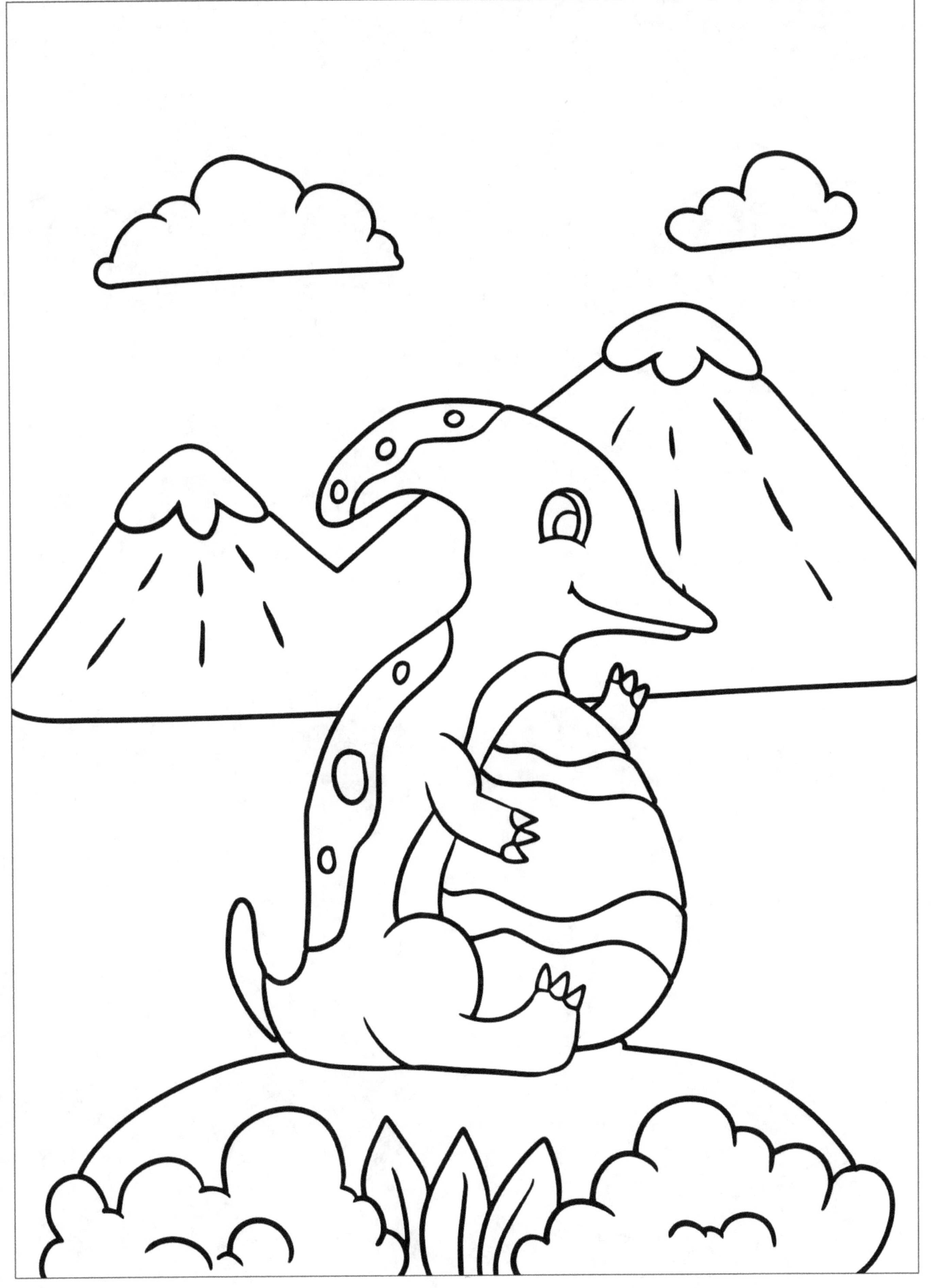

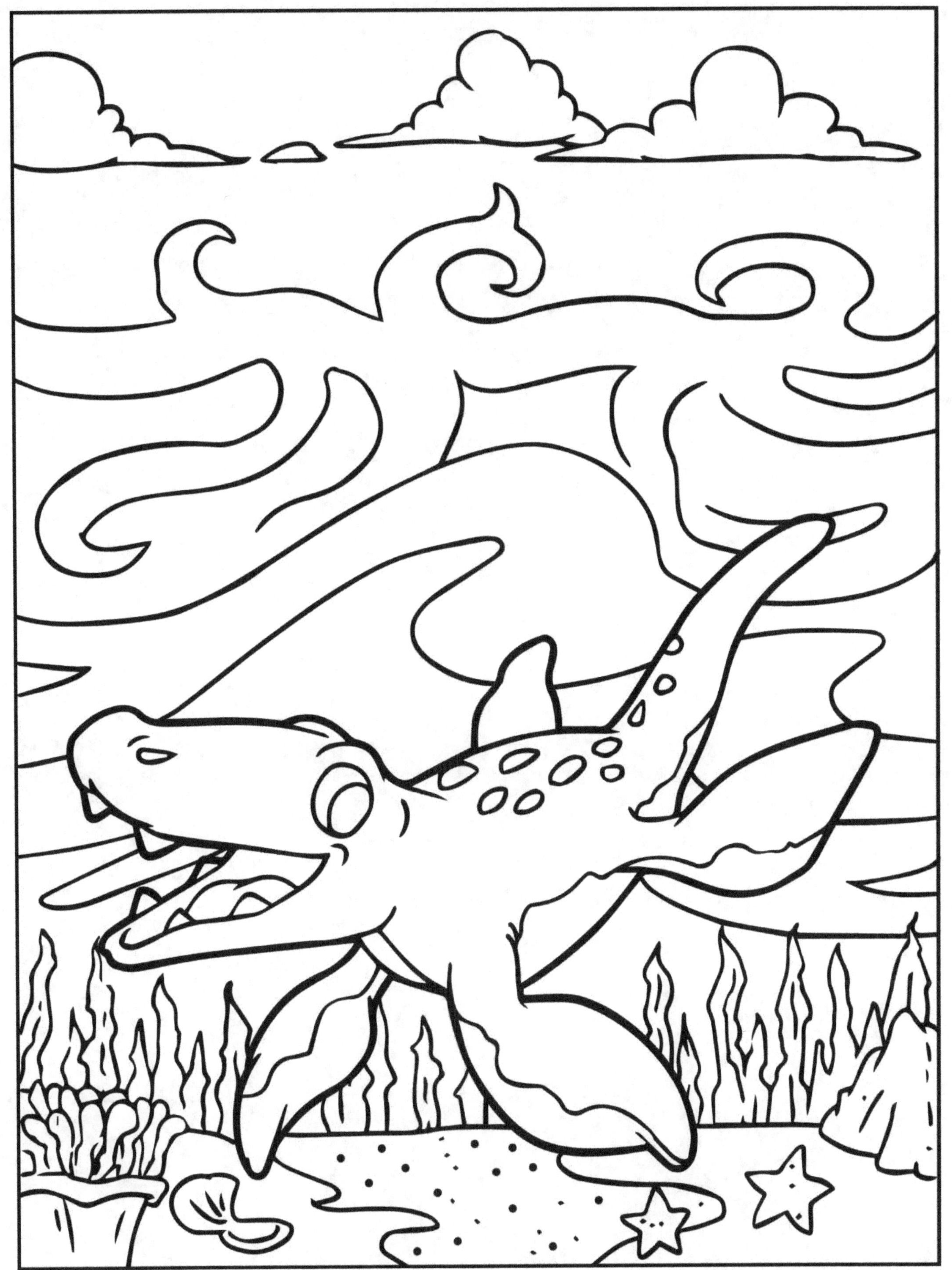

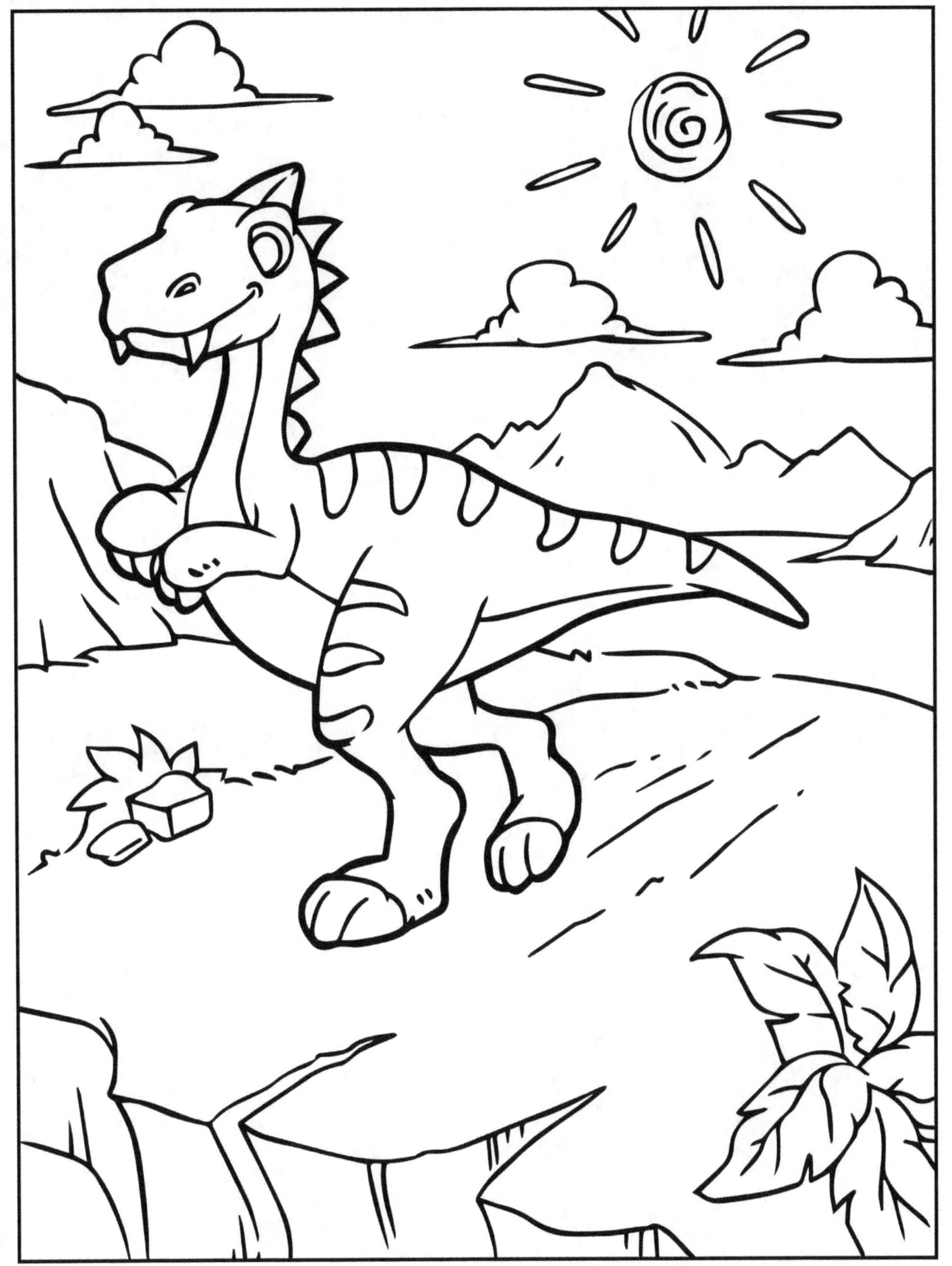

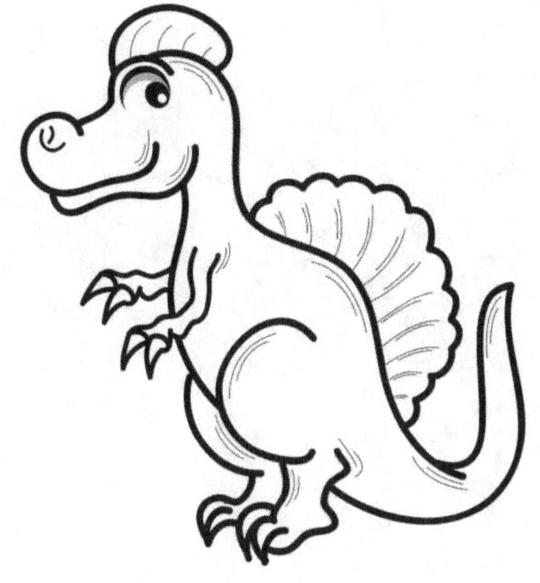

Thank You
&
Happy Coloring

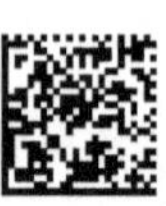
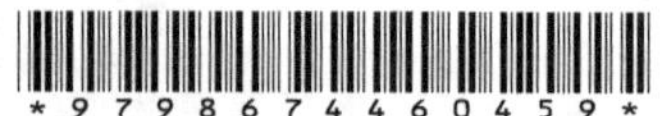